BLOOD MONEY

CAROL EVERETT
WITH JACK SHAW

MULTNOMAH PRESS

BLOOD MONEY
© 1992 by Carol Everett with Jack Shaw

Published by Multnomah Press Books
Questar Publishers, Inc.
Sisters, Oregon

Originally published in hardcover as *The Scarlet Lady*,
© 1991 by Carol Everett with Jack Shaw

Cover Photography by Greg Schneider

Printed in the United States of America

International Standard Book Number: 0-88070-548-5

*Dedicated to the 35,000 mothers to whom I sold abortions
and their 35,000 unborn babies.*

*To the 35,000 fathers and other family members
affected by these abortions.*

*To Tom, the father of my unborn child,
who participated in our abortion unaware
that he, too, would be victimized.*

*And to my unborn daughter, Heidi, and all the unborn
who face her fate unless their cries are heard—
"Let me live! Let me live!"*

ACKNOWLEDGMENTS

•••

I would like to thank my parents for giving me life. Though they have not approved of all my choices, they have loved me. And now, as we adjust to life without my father, my mother is becoming one of my best friends.

I would like to thank my living children, Kelly and Joe Bob, and my daughter-in-law, Carol, Jr., who love me just as I am. Though my children have had to live with my many mistakes, they have loved me through it all and are now my strongest supporters in the pro-life work.

Thank you, John and Ardella Shoop, Nelson and Stephanie Cook, Barbara Lee, Valerie Syzmaniak, Richard and Jill Bowles, Jerry and Karen Green, and many other friends of my new life who have prayed for me, loved me unconditionally, and stood by me during my metamorphosis from abortionist to pro-lifer.

My gratitude to George Dulany, Jr., Ethelyn English, Barbara Schlapfer, and Donna West, our dedicated office staff who lovingly supported us throughout the development of this book.

Thank you, Jennifer Moore, for your long hours of labor, for believing in this book, and for encouraging me as I struggled through my emotions in committing my life to paper. Through your eyes, I saw that others could be helped by my experiences. Thank you for becoming my cherished friend in the process. Thank you, Rusty and Heather, for allowing your wife and mother to devote untold hours to this project.

Most of all I would like to thank Jack and Gwen Shaw, who have loved me, accepted me, and taught me by example and word the Christian way of life. They have been available to me since the moment I uttered that prayer of salvation. They are retraining me—Jack, the godly man, teaching Christian truths, grounding me in my new understanding of the love of God and helping me in the work the Lord has for me; and Gwen, the example of the godly woman I want to be.

As we finish this book, I would like to thank Gwen and the Shaw children— Wendy, Rhonda, and David—for their patient and loving support while Jack and I have written this book.

And thank You, Lord, for redeeming me from the miry pit and for Your redeeming love that continues to work in my life.

CONTENTS

AUTHOR'S NOTE

••

All of the stories in this book are true. In some, the names have been changed. In all instances, the events and conversations accurately reflect factual situations.

This is the truth. This is my story.

1

••••••••••••••••••••••••

THE NEIMAN-MARCUS
OF THE INDUSTRY

D R. HARVEY JOHNSON—"Harvey" to me—appeared at my
office door. "Carol, come back to recovery with me," he said with
a nod, extending his hand toward me.

I hurried to join him in the hallway, where he slipped an arm
around my shoulder, as he did so often. "What's wrong, Harvey?"

"Sheryl passed a clot. She's bleeding heavily, but she'll be all right."
He spoke in a low, quiet tone.

We turned the corner into the recovery room and walked to
Sheryl's bed. Becky and Connie, both LPNs, stood over her. Her pants
were off and she was lying in a pool of blood. The bed was soaked with
blood, the privacy curtains were splashed with it, and even the wall had
blood on it. Despite being an operating room technician, I was
shocked by the scene. I had never seen so much blood in all my life.

I could feel Harvey's hand tighten on the back of my neck. He
moved to Sheryl's side, directing his comments to one of the nurses.
"Connie, massage her fundus. This will close her uterus down after all
the clots are out, and the bleeding will stop." As he spoke, he gently ap-
plied pressure on Sheryl's small abdomen and, with a circular motion,
massaged the top of her uterus, known as the fundus.

My medical experience kicked in and I touched Sheryl's arm.
"How are you doing, Sheryl?"

"Okay, I guess." She sounded weak.

"Everything will be all right. I'll stay here with you. After we get
you cleaned up we'll bring Bob back, too." I nodded to Becky, who
seemed relieved to have someone else in charge.

In January 1982 we were a clean clinic, a top-notch operation. We
considered ourselves the Neiman-Marcus of the abortion industry—
we'd never had a single complication, not even a major infection.
Harvey and I had accomplished things our competition could only

dream of doing. Our confidence in our ability was high; our judgments seemed almost infallible. Our doctors were Ob-Gyn's—all but one board-certified. But suddenly we faced a major complication, and we were vulnerable.

Sheryl first had come into the clinic on Wednesday morning and had filled out the usual forms; she indicated she was eighteen weeks pregnant. The rate for an abortion at that point was three hundred seventy-five dollars, which she paid in cash. However, in the examining room Dr. Johnson discovered she actually was *twenty* weeks along. He informed her that an abortion would now cost an additional one hundred twenty-five dollars. Sheryl became agitated. So did Harvey, who brought the problem to me to straighten out.

"Carol, we need a policy for sizing patients who are over twelve weeks pregnant before they pay. This woman got all the way to the back having paid three hundred seventy-five dollars for eighteen weeks, but she's actually twenty weeks along. She's upset because she doesn't have the additional one hundred twenty-five dollars. You talk to her and get her money so we can get this done." He handed me the chart and walked away, motioning briskly to a young woman who had just slipped into the hall from an examining room. As clinic administrator, I knew what to do.

"Sheryl, please come into my office and have a seat while I look at your chart." She sat nervously in the chair I indicated, glancing up only when I spoke again. "You thought you were eighteen weeks pregnant, but Dr. Johnson found you to be twenty weeks when he did the pelvic examination. At this stage the cost is more, and you will have to pay another hundred twenty-five dollars. Do you have the money?"

"No. We could barely come up with three seventy-five. My boyfriend, Bob, and I live together with my two-year-old son. I have another son who's seventeen, but he lives with my mother in Nebraska. Bob and I both work, but it takes everything we make. I don't know how we can get any more money. We're already using part of our rent payment for this month. Can we work out some kind of payment plan? We'll pay you, I swear." She kept wringing her hands as she tried desperately to convince me to help her.

It didn't work. I knew my job and sentiment wasn't part of it. I put down the chart and looked her in the eye. "No, we are not allowed to make pay-out agreements," I said sympathetically, "and we can't do the procedure until you have the rest of the money. I must stress the urgency, however, because the price keeps going up each week you wait. The charge at twenty-four weeks is seven hundred and fifty, rather than five hundred. You need to find the money as quickly as you can."

I watched her shoulders slump. I got up, walked around to the front of my desk, and leaned back against it. "Surely you have a family member who could lend you the money, don't you?" I coaxed. "What about a friend? Do you have friends who could lend you part of the money? Perhaps some family members or friends could loan you twenty-five or even fifty dollars each."

"I can't think of anyone who could. I'm so upset," she stammered. "I really don't know. What are you going to do about the three hundred seventy-five dollars I have already paid you?"

"We'll just hold it until Friday evening. I'm sure you'll find the money. Go home and talk to Bob about it. I'm sure you can come up with the money by Friday. If you can, call me back and we'll be able to do the procedure Friday evening for the same price—five hundred dollars. But remember, the longer you wait, the more it will cost. Sheryl, this is such a critical time. Just come up with the extra one hundred twenty-five dollars and we will take care of everything on Friday." She stood up and I walked her to the door, patting her shoulder reassuringly.

"I Have the Money"

Sheryl returned Friday, as I expected. She was very shy when she walked into my office; it was after 7:00 P.M. "I have the money. Is it too late to do it tonight?"

"No, Sheryl, it's not," I said with a smile. "We can do it tonight, but before we start, I have something for you." I closed the door to my office and gave her a coupon I had clipped out of the newspaper for her. "This will give you a ten percent discount so you'll have some grocery money until you get paid again." I hugged her and then directed her to the front to pay, while we waited for her chart to be pulled.

I knew Sheryl would be in recovery a long time because of the length of her pregnancy. Now I had to rush things along because recovery-room nurses were not cheap. I had a date later that night and a long day ahead of me on Saturday.

"We need to do this procedure as soon as possible so Sheryl can recover while the other abortions are being done," I told the staff. "We don't want to be here all night."

When Sheryl came back to the operating room, she said, "I'm scared. I don't know why. This is not my first abortion—I had another one some time ago. But this time I'm really scared."

I had an intuition that Sheryl had been hurt a lot in her life. She seemed so helpless against a cruel world. I wanted to protect her, to help another hurting woman. I stopped what I was doing and took her hand. "Don't worry, Sheryl. Everything is going to be all right. I'll go through the procedure with you. I'll be here to help. It will all be over soon, you'll see."

On the procedure table I became aware of how petite Sheryl was. About five feet tall, she was stunningly beautiful—not blatantly sexy, just naturally beautiful. Her skin was a flawless, creamy white. She had blonde hair and blue eyes...eyes that betrayed her fright.

Sheryl was very cooperative. She slid her tiny body down to the edge of the table, placing her pelvis in just the right position to permit the baby's body parts to fall into a cold, stainless steel pan without making a mess.

I held her hand and coached her through the procedure as I had learned to do in Lamaze classes. I used what I learned in those child-birth classes to coach women through the abortion procedure, helping to limit the screaming.

"Take a deep breath, Sheryl. Everything is going to be all right," I said.

After all, I reasoned, who better to do Sheryl's abortion than the man whom I had trusted to do my own abortion? Mine had gone smoothly, with no medical complications, and I believed Sheryl would be just fine, too. I was helping the best abortionist I knew to perform abortions on other women—I guess I thought Harvey Johnson was the best abortionist money could buy.

"Take another deep breath, Sheryl. Let's count to ten before you take another one. It'll help slow down your body. I'm going to pinch your elbow. Concentrate on your elbow."

I can still remember Sheryl's eyes. Even today I'm not sure what I saw. Fear? Pain? Both? Her eyes were haunted, almost empty; yet some emotion—deeper than the emptiness—was reflected there.

I looked down to see how the procedure was going. Everything seemed to be all right. The arms and legs of the baby, the first parts to come out, were in the pan. Harvey reached for the body.

Usually, I was the one who held the baby motionless in the uterus, using a technique called the Hanson maneuver, whereby the technician's hand is on the fundus and the contents of the uterus. This time Leslie assisted, while I held Sheryl's hand.

Using the Hanson maneuver, the technician can tell the doctor where the body parts are, quietly directing him: "The head is here, the buttocks here, and the arms and legs here." If the abortionist performs the maneuver himself, he can tell where the parts are.

I liked to help Dr. Johnson, and performing the Hanson maneuver was my way of aiding him in the abortion procedure. Harvey trusted my help because of previous procedures we had done together. In one case, he thought he was finished, even though I could still feel something inside the uterus. I insisted, and, in order to placate me, he reached back in, only to pull out the baby's bottom. Had he stopped without checking further, we would have had a major complication on our hands. I hoped nothing like that would happen with the woman now on the table.

"Take another deep breath, Sheryl. Really deep. Fill your lungs. Now hold it for a few seconds. Slowly release your breath. It's just about over. Are you doing okay?"

Sheryl nodded her head.

Dr. Johnson had gotten the baby's body out by now and was searching for the head. This largest part of the baby's body is usually the last to come out. The head must be located and crushed before it can pass through the cervix. Usually it is first deflated—by suctioning out the brain and all the other contents.

"Suction, please," Harvey said, but Leslie was ahead of him; the suction was in his hand almost before he asked. A good nurse/assistant anticipates what the abortionist will ask for next and is ready. She turned on the machine, and the roar of the motor startled Sheryl.

"Be still, Sheryl," I urged. "That's the sound of normal procedure equipment. Take another deep breath. It's almost over."

Dr. Johnson handed the suction tube back to Leslie and once again used forceps to probe for the head. I saw the muscles of his right arm tighten and knew what that meant: He had located the head and was crushing it. Harvey used to joke about getting tennis elbow from this technique, and his right arm was actually slightly larger than his left.

"Take a real deep breath, Sheryl—right now." I tried to ready Sheryl for the pain of the crushed head passing through her cervix.

Sheryl gasped and turned pale, but she did not utter a single word.

Harvey spoke first to Leslie, then to his patient: "Suction, one last time. It's all over, Sheryl. Everything is fine."

Harvey stood up and with bloody gloves picked up the tray containing the baby's torn body. Leslie opened the door, and Harvey went to Central Supply while I pulled Sheryl up on the table.

"Put your feet down, and push back," I directed. "We'll get you dressed and into the recovery room. In a few minutes you can have a Coke."

Leslie entered and handed me a sanitary pad which I helped Sheryl place between her legs. She then helped Sheryl dress while I went to talk to Harvey.

I found him still in Central Supply, checking to be certain he had removed all the parts. He reconstructed the baby's body on an underpad while he talked.

"Fredi is waiting for me at Ninfa's," he said. "We're in the mood for Mexican food and margaritas tonight."

I didn't ask questions. It was unusual for Harvey to drink, but he had been doing it more and more lately. At that time, I blamed his girlfriend, Fredi, but now I wonder if he might have had another reason. Could he have been struggling with our recent decision to do second- and third-trimester abortions?

I must admit we started doing late-term abortions at my insistence. We needed to expand our services, and the only way to do it was to do late-term procedures—the ones we called "bigger" abortions. I also wanted to utilize the building all week long; after all, the rent was paid for all seven days. Why not use the clinic every day?

"You look nice tonight, Carol. Are you dressed up for anything special?" Harvey asked. He had accounted for all the body parts and now started to put the baby's body down the disposal. I turned it on for him so he wouldn't get blood on the switch.

"Yes, I have a date tonight with Kerry," I replied. "I hope we can get out of here early. We're going dancing." I turned off the disposal. We worked so well together, Harvey and I; our camaraderie was comfortable and reassuring. "I'll see you before you leave," I told him. "I'm going back to my office to finish some paperwork." We parted easily, eager to finish our work for the evening.

Since Sheryl was the last big one for the night, I could get some work done without worrying about the other procedures. Leslie, Becky, and Connie all had plans for the evening, too, so they would move Harvey quickly from room to room, finishing the rest of the abortions.

A Major Complication

I was in my office figuring the day's profits when Harvey interrupted me with news of Sheryl's problem. The amount of blood in the room scared me. Suddenly, we weren't looking so top-notch. We faced our first major complication.

Medically, Harvey was in control of the situation; emotionally, he was shaken. He and the nurses continued to massage Sheryl's uterus until the bleeding slowed. But for some reason he didn't put her back on the table for another pelvic examination to determine the source of the bleeding.

Harvey and I stepped outside the recovery room to talk. By this time, we were both calm again. He looked at his watch. "I'm leaving to meet Fredi at Ninfa's," he said. "I'll call back, and I have my beeper on if you need me. Sheryl will be fine. Just be sure to keep massaging her uterus until the bleeding stops. When her vital signs are stable, dismiss her. I'll see you in the morning." His big hand squeezed my arm one last time and I returned to Sheryl's side.

One LPN continued to massage her uterus, and the bleeding diminished considerably. We moved Sheryl to another bed and cleaned the room as best we could. When everything was presentable, I took Bob back to be with Sheryl.

Bob hovered over her; he seemed to really care, perhaps even to love Sheryl. I wondered why they weren't married. They didn't seem to have the same scars carried by Harvey, myself, and the other divorced people in my world. Somehow there was an innocence about their relationship, rather than the anger I might have expected.

For a moment I felt jealous of Sheryl's beauty and her relationship with Bob. They had no complicated goals, no driving ambition to get rich; their lives seemed simple. Not like mine—I was alone, pushing to be wealthy. They had something I wanted more than anything else—an honest, caring relationship.

In many ways, Sheryl and Bob were just an average couple having an abortion. They were having financial problems and believed abortion was the simplest way to go on with their lives—with one less liability. This abortion would give them a financial reprieve. Soon, perhaps, they could get married and live happily ever after.

By now the front office personnel had balanced the books and closed for the evening, while I stayed with Sheryl and Bob. The telephones were transferred to the answering service, eliminating disturbances.

At about nine o'clock we ran out of sanitary napkins. I rushed out of the clinic and called my date. "Kerry, we've had a complication at the clinic. I have to go back and make sure the patient is okay. I'm sorry."

"That's okay, Carol," he responded.

"Can you come by the house later?"

"About what time?"

"Not before eleven-thirty."

"Sure."

"I'll see you later, then. I have to go." I picked up some sanitary napkins and hurried back to the clinic.

By the time I returned, Sheryl's blood pressure had dropped very low. I paged Harvey. He called, but when the answering service picked up, he assumed everything was all right.

Sheryl and Bob were unconcerned about her low blood pressure. "Can't I go home now?" she pleaded with me. "My blood pressure is always low. Don't be concerned about it. I don't feel good, but I know I'll feel better after I'm in my own bed. Please let me go home now."

Her blood pressure was low, but stable, and the bleeding was under control. At about eleven o'clock, I released her. "Sheryl, you can go home, but if anything—I mean *anything*—unusual happens, call our emergency number at once."

"We'll call if anything happens," she assured me.

Connie wheeled Sheryl to the front door in a wheelchair while Bob went to get the car. I walked out with her. "Sheryl, call me in the morning to let me know how you're doing. Call us tonight if you have even the slightest question. Please don't hesitate to call. No question is foolish when it involves your health."

Relieved to be going, Sheryl and Bob promised they would call— even if it seemed like a minor problem. "Thanks for everything, Carol," Sheryl said, smiling. "We promise to call if we need you tonight. And I'll call you when I wake up in the morning." I closed their car door and they drove away.

We watched them leave.

"She didn't look good, Carol," Connie commented.

"I know, but what else could we do?" I shook my head, then walked back into the clinic to lock up.

I rushed home to meet Kerry. The doorbell rang, and I forgot about Sheryl.

I was ironing my uniform when the telephone rang Saturday morning at six. Harvey's voice was subdued.

"Sheryl Mason is dead."

I felt the color draining from my face.

"No, Harvey, she's not dead. She can't be."

"Carol, I'm here with her at Presbyterian. She's on life support right now. We're forcing fluids, but she's going to die. It's only a matter of time. This one is dead."

"She's only thirty-two years old! She can't die. She was going to call if there was a problem." I searched for something that would change what he was telling me. It just couldn't be true.

Harvey's voice sounded tired. "Her boyfriend called me this morning at about three and told me Sheryl was cramping heavily. I told him to put her in a tub of hot water. He called back a little later to say she was unconscious. I told him to get her to Presbyterian Hospital Emergency Room at once, and I would meet them there. When she arrived, I started intravenous fluids and a blood transfusion...but she's gone."

"Harvey, she can't be dead! She's going to be all right".... I was arguing with myself more than Harvey.

"I'm sorry, Carol," he said.

This couldn't be happening. We were supposed to be helping women—not killing them!

Silence replaced conversation.

Finally I asked, "What are we going to do?"

Harvey's reply was immediate. "We're going to go on as if nothing happened. Patients are scheduled at 8:00 A.M. How many do we have on the schedule this morning?"

"Twenty-eight," I said, forcing my mind to focus.

"When you get in," Harvey said, "find Sheryl's chart. Keep it in your office so no one else can see it. I'll be late—it'll be after nine before I can get there. I'll keep you informed. Be ready when I get there."

"I've got to pick up groceries for lunch at the clinic," I said, trying to keep my voice calm, "but I'll be there as soon as I can. Goodbye."

A vast emptiness, an indescribable void, engulfed me.

Moving like a robot, I finished ironing, dressed, stopped by the grocery store, and then arrived at the clinic. Connie greeted me in the hall. "I tried to call you at home last night, but your answering machine picked up. I wondered about Sheryl—if we should have released her. Did you hear from her?"

"No," I answered. It was the truth. I didn't hear from Sheryl; Harvey did.

"She must be all right then, or we would have heard," Connie continued.

"Yes," I lied.

In addition to being Harvey's girlfriend, Fredi was also our bookkeeper. Later, she and I sat in the front office. I found myself staring out the window. Connie walked in and said, "Carol, you look like you lost your best friend."

"I'm fine, Connie."

Fredi walked over and hugged me. We had never been on friendly terms, so I must have looked terrible if even Fredi thought I needed a hug!

I went through the motions of getting the morning's patients ready for the doctor, thankful for the good help we had. I couldn't concentrate.

Finally, Harvey came in the back door. I rushed to him for some word of comfort, some sign of hope. He looked terrible, but I desperately needed to be held, as if that would make things better. He held me for a minute, sensing the urgency in me. Then he asked, "How many are in so far?"

"Twenty, and we're ready to go."

"Let's do it. You know I have to train John Miller today."

"Yes, I know. He's already here." Dr. John Miller was a psychiatrist who had done abortions for another chain of clinics. But now Harvey had to teach him our way—the *right* way. How ironic! Today, of all days!

"Let's show him how it's done." Harvey moved quickly down the hall, his attitude all business.

We entered the first room. I wasn't ready to leave Harvey yet. I needed him, needed his strength—something, anything—to help me go on...just for today. But he was cold, offering me nothing.

I checked the front waiting room to see how many were in. I wondered if Harvey would work so fast that I would have difficulty keeping the instruments "turned"—cleaned and re-sterilized after each procedure, but cool enough for him to use for the next abortion. Today he was uncharacteristically slow in training Dr. Miller. *Thank heaven!* I thought. I was slow, too.

Throughout the morning my mind was screaming—at first in remorse for what had happened to Sheryl: *What if I had died and left my two children without their mother? Sheryl's children don't have a mother; they're orphans now.*

Then in fearful self-pity: *How am I going to make a living now, if the clinic closes? I've put all my energy into the abortion business for the past three years and it's just now beginning to pay off.*

I've finally reached the point that I don't have to worry about money to send the kids to college. Joe Bob is graduating this May. I promised Kelly and Joe Bob that if they would work during high school, they wouldn't have to work in college.

I've worked all my life to be able to give them the things their father would have given them if I had stayed in the marriage. Now what am I going to do? I have all my eggs in this basket, and it's falling apart. There's no time for me to establish myself in another profession before Joe Bob goes to college.

We won't be able to go on. The clinic's reputation is ruined! Even if we aren't forced to close the clinic, no one will come to us for an abortion. We just killed a woman!

Eventually, reason and routine took hold. I forced myself to think rationally.

Concentrate on today, Carol. Get through this day and deal with the future later.

I had lunch with Dr. Miller, our new abortionist. I wanted desperately to tell him, "I need help. A woman died this morning from an abortion we did here last night." But of course, I couldn't.

Instead, I listened to him talk—a doctor who thought he knew it all. "Every woman deserves the right to an abortion. I grew up with Baptist parents, and they don't believe in abortion. I've had to fight for my beliefs and the rights of women." So that was how he saw himself—as the champion of women.

If you only knew the truth, I thought. *This clinic will close. We can't talk to you about a job. You're wasting your time here today.*

Maybe We'll Be All Right

Somehow, I got through the day and rushed home. The phone was ringing. It was Harvey. "Are you all right?"

"I'm as good as I can be under the circumstances. How are you?" It was good to hear his voice.

"I'm fine. Fredi and I were just talking; we have each other to hold on to—but you've got nobody. How about coming over tomorrow afternoon at about two to talk this out?" he asked.

"Yes, I'll be there. But can you tell me more about what happened last night?"

"What do you want to know?"

"Why did she die?"

"I don't know the cause of death. I've talked to the coroner's office, and he'll let me know as soon as he does the autopsy."

"How is her family holding up?" I asked.

"Bob is in a state of shock. His parents were with him at the hospital. He asked me to call Sheryl's mother in Nebraska. She was upset—even angry. When she asked why Sheryl died, I told her it was from female complications. She said, `She died from an abortion, didn't she?'"

"What did you say?" I was frightened.

"I told her `No,'" Harvey answered quickly. "Bob didn't want her family to know about the abortion, and that may be what saves us. We have to support Bob now, so he'll help us. If we can keep this out of the newspapers, I think we'll be all right.

"No one at Presbyterian will report us," Harvey continued, "with one exception. One of the nurses has a brother-in-law who's a doctor practicing in Garland. I talked to her, and I hope she doesn't tell him. If she doesn't, I don't think news of it will get back to Garland. And if it doesn't get back to Garland, my private practice won't be affected. Then, if it doesn't get into the papers, it won't affect the clinic." I had to admit—Harvey had thought it all out.

"All we have to be concerned about is the cause of death," he finished. "If that's all right, we'll be okay."

"Do you mean we'll be able to keep the clinic open?" I asked in astonishment.

"Yes, of course. We can go on."

I couldn't believe my ears! He said what I wanted—with all my heart—to hear. Was it possible that we could kill a woman, then go on as if nothing ever happened? Was the industry that unregulated? Could Harvey Johnson get other doctors to cover for him even in the case of a woman's death? Maybe my life wasn't over; I would be able to send my kids to college after all. Perhaps, just perhaps, there was hope for going on, hope I hadn't dared expect.

After my conversation with Harvey, my children, Kelly and Joe Bob, joined me in our living room. Kelly worked part-time as a receptionist/counselor at the clinic and had been working Friday evening when Sheryl came in. She already knew we had a problem with the procedure. "Kelly, do you remember Sheryl Mason, the big one we had trouble with last night?"

"Yes."

I took a deep breath before my next words. I decided to be honest with them. "Well, she died early this morning. Right now we don't know why. We don't have the autopsy results but she probably died from the abortion. We have to keep this confidential. I need you both, now. I don't know what's going to happen."

"What do you *think* will happen, Mom?" Kelly asked.

"I really don't know, baby. I hope there isn't anything in either of the Sunday papers. If we can keep it out of the newspapers, we may be all right. I'm going to meet with Harvey tomorrow afternoon and talk about everything. I'm not sure we can go on. Hug me," I begged. "I love you both. Thanks for standing by me."

The three of us hugged. I was so glad I could discuss the situation with my children. *They'll stand by me,* I reasoned. I prayed it was true.

Kerry and I had another date Saturday night. As we sat on the hearth before the fireplace, I said, "Kerry, I just don't know what happened. We're supposed to be helping women, but this one died."

"Carol, people die from all sorts of unexpected things. Think about it. As a policeman, I see people die all the time. Women still die from childbirth occasionally. Don't worry about it. Think of all the women you've helped. Everything will be all right," he reassured.

"Hold me, Kerry," I said, leaning into him.

"Everything will be fine. You'll see," he soothed. Oh, how I wanted to believe him!

Sunday afternoon at two, I was on Harvey's doorstep, eager to finish our discussion.

"What's happened since we talked?" I asked when he answered the door.

"I talked with the coroner's office. He hasn't done the autopsy yet but he'll call as soon as he determines the cause of death. I told him we'd send our medical records for his chart." Harvey looked closely at me. "We have to change the blood pressure readings on Sheryl's chart to normal ones. Fredi and I have discussed it and think it'll be easy to cut along the lines, recopy the chart, and no one will ever know the difference. Can you go over to the clinic with us this afternoon to do that?"

"No, I have other plans," I lied. I was desperate, but I wasn't willing to falsify medical records. "How's Bob today?"

"He's fine. He's going to Nebraska for the funeral and will be back later in the week. If he doesn't tell Sheryl's mother, I think we'll get by without a lawsuit. Bob feels pretty guilty right now. He blames himself for Sheryl's pregnancy and for bringing her in for the abortion. We can use that to our advantage. We just have to be there for him for a while. His mother is with him, which will help us, I believe. She keeps telling him he did the best he could." Harvey leaned back in his chair.

"What did we do wrong, Harvey?" I asked.

Harvey shrugged his shoulders, then leaned forward. "Carol, if you deliver enough babies, a mother will die. Women still die in childbirth. We've been very lucky to have avoided a major complication before now. Our number was just up. We can't worry about it. We have to go on. If we can make it without a story getting in the newspapers, we'll be okay."

"What about the cause of death?"

"That could be a concern. However, the coroner knows me by reputation. He'll call me Monday or Tuesday with the cause of death. I'll call you as soon as I know anything."

"Could they file charges?" I had to know.

"Don't even think about it!" he answered quickly. "Check the newspapers in the morning. I'll call you between surgery cases and see if anything comes up." He patted my hand. "Carol, don't worry. Everything is going to be fine."

I left Harvey's house, still in shock, still unconvinced everything was going to be fine. After all—Sheryl Mason was alive two days ago. Now she lay cold and dead—because I sold her on having the abortion and showed her how to get the extra money she needed. I didn't want my usual twenty-five-dollar commission for this one.

Monday morning came, and there was no mention in the newspapers of the abortion-related death. Not even the dignity of an obituary.

Harvey's phone call greeted me as I entered my office. "Fredi and I went to the clinic and took care of the chart," he said. "We brought the blood pressure up to normal. It really looked good. We sent a copy of the records to the coroner's office. The changed chart is in the center drawer of your desk. Hide it somewhere so no one can find it," he instructed.

"Okay, I'll put it under the files in my top right-hand drawer," I said. Under the files—and under the Bible I kept in that drawer.

Tuesday morning arrived—still nothing in the papers.

Harvey telephoned. "The coroner called with the results of the autopsy. The cause of death was hemorrhaging from a cervical tear."

I went numb.

We could have saved Sheryl's life! my mind screamed. We only needed to have sutured her cervix. We had everything we needed in the clinic to save Sheryl's life, with one exception—a doctor willing to take the time to re-examine his patient to determine the cause of the bleeding. But he had a date, and the margaritas were waiting.

Sheryl Mason's death was unnecessary—that much was clear. Even a first-year intern would have checked for the source of such profuse bleeding, but Dr. Harvey Johnson diagnosed without a physical examination—and diagnosed wrongly.

This doctor, a man I too had trusted with my life, was not trustworthy. Yes, it was only one mistake, but a deadly one.

I firmly purposed to watch him more closely in the future. Regaining my composure, I continued the conversation.

"Harvey, what's going to happen?"

"Nothing, I hope. You might get out your prayer rug on this one, though."

I scanned the paper on Wednesday. Still nothing. So far, so good… The same thing on Thursday….

"I think we're okay, Carol."

Okay? Maybe so—but we were no longer the Neiman-Marcus of the abortion industry.

By now I wondered if such a thing as a high-class abortion clinic were even possible. Regardless of the efficiency of our operation, the professionalism of our staff, the effectiveness of our marketing—could anyone do what we had done to Sheryl Mason and still consider themselves anything other than sleazy and brutal?

How had I ended up here? How had that fair-haired girl from San Saba, Texas gotten involved with a business that could kill women it was supposed to be helping—creating a pool of blood deep enough to drown her guilty soul? Was I strong enough to succeed in this role I had taken upon myself?

2

CHILDHOOD LESSONS

MOTHER TOLD ME she wanted to surprise Daddy with the good news. "Sonny, I'm pregnant," she informed him. "We're going to have a baby in December."

For some reason, Daddy was not surprised. "I know you're pregnant; you've missed two periods," he replied. "It's going to be a girl."

"She'll be arriving near Christmas, if not on Christmas!" Mother exclaimed.

"Carol should be her name, then," Daddy concluded.

"I'd like to name a girl after my sister, Nan. What do you think about the name Carol Nan?" Mother asked.

"I like it. That'll be her name."

On December 22, 1944, after two years of marriage, Sonny and Dorothy Gage received their daughter, Carol Nan Gage. My father was a Navy cook stationed in Orange, Texas; two days before my birth, he was shipped out to sea. He learned of my birth over the ship's loudspeaker.

While Daddy was overseas, Mother and I went to live with her parents and my Aunt Nan and Uncle Max in Houston.

Mother stayed at home with me while the other adults worked. I was a breast-fed baby, watched over very carefully by my mother and grandparents.

Always dressed perfectly, I was the center of attention and the family entertainment—especially when everyone returned home from work. Adored by all, I was given everything I wanted.

Through the years, I've often heard the words, "You were such a good baby. We didn't need to correct you because you were so good!" I suppose I provided a certain amount of joy for a family longing to have their hearts lightened, especially during the war.

Mother often showed me a picture of Daddy to make sure I would know him when he returned from overseas. "This is your daddy. Isn't he handsome? He loves you so much. When he gets home, you'll love him, too."

He returned on December 11, 1945. When he was discharged from the Navy, we returned to my parent's hometown of San Saba, Texas.

Life seemed good then. Daddy and I were busy getting to know each other. I soon learned that all I had to say was, "Daddy, Daddy," in order to capture his undivided attention.

But I was unaware of the storm that was brewing. Mother was feeling left out—not so much because of Daddy's developing relationship with me, but because of his sense of responsibility to his mother.

When Daddy was seventeen, his father died. To help support the family, Daddy quit school and got a job at a grocery store—making seven dollars a week. When he returned from the Navy, my grandmother was still on his mental list of dependents. My mother deeply disliked sharing Daddy with his mother and the rest of his family. She wasn't getting the attention a young bride expected to have from her returning hero.

I don't think Mother blamed me, but I'm convinced she did blame my father's family. From early childhood and throughout my life, I often heard Mother say things to Daddy like, "You always put your family first, ahead of us." And so, I learned about jealousy as I learned about my father.

By the age of two I felt like a real "queen"—partly because I was asked to be the little "queen" of the San Saba May Fete, along with two-year-old Sonny Berrien who would be the little "king." I was full of life.

Everyone made sure that life revolved around me. I may have been a "joy" to my family, but I was spoiled rotten. My daddy's philosophy of child development was simple: "You don't start correcting children until they're two. You don't tell them 'no' until then." So—early on, I established my own boundaries.

The time finally came when Daddy, my big "king," hurt his little "queen" for the first time. I was only two years old, and we lived in a duplex next door to Daddy's brother and his family.

"Carol Nan and I are going outside for a walk," Daddy informed Mother as she was cleaning the kitchen. Standing in the sun and holding my father's hand made me feel very happy.

Some friends drove by and stopped for a visit. Suddenly, a wasp came out of the shrubbery and stung my eyelid. I turned and reached out, screaming, "Daddy! Daddy!"

He slapped me!

Confused and hurting, I screamed louder.

Hearing my screams, Mother rushed out of the house and rescued me. "What happened? Move your hand and let me see your eye. Oh, Carol Nan, you've been stung! It's okay. It's going to be okay. Let's go inside and put something on it."

I felt pain from my eye, but I felt much deeper pain within my confused two-year-old heart.

Strength Is Power

Years later, I recognized attitudes that were formed in that brief childhood encounter with my father. I thought I was Daddy's perfect girl. But, for some reason beyond my understanding, I had failed. What did I do wrong—what caused him to slap me? Maybe I would just have to try harder to please him, I reasoned.

I also learned that the strong endure pain. They don't cry out—lest their weakness summon punishment. I would be strong!

In San Saba, Daddy worked in the same grocery store he had worked in before he went into the Navy. To make extra money, he butchered cattle at night for the meat market. Mother and I often went with him.

We watched him put the animals in a building with a concrete floor that sloped to a drain in the center. He closed the door and shot the cow. Then we would go in and watch him pull the cow off the floor and hang it from the ceiling. I can still see the rivers of blood running down that drain. I learned to accept that blood as a necessary part of Daddy's job. Daddy dressed each cow, quartered it, took it to the grocery store, and hung it in the store's cooler.

Even as a young child I loved to be in charge, to win. When I played with my cousin Nancy, I can remember standing on her side of the driveway dividing our family's duplex and insisting, "Stay over on your side of the driveway, Nancy. The driveway is mine to this line."

Of course, seventy-five percent of the driveway was always mine!

Nancy stood on the tiny strip of driveway I conceded to her, and cried. I loved it.

All my possessions had to be bigger and better, including my swing set. Daddy built mine out of pipe, set in concrete. It was taller than a normal child's swing set, which enabled me to swing higher, to enjoy the thrill of conquering new heights.

I remember telling Nancy, "Since you don't have a swing set, come swing on my big swing set." Then I pushed her as high as I could, hoping to scare her.

When I was six, my parents told me, "You're going to get a baby— your very own baby." They didn't want me to be jealous, so they told me it would be mine.

Mother said, "If it's a boy, his name will be Calvin Jefferson, after your daddy and grandfather. But if it's a girl, you get to choose the name."

"I'll give her a good name," I assured them, "one she'll like. Her name will be Diane." Two weeks before my sister was born, someone else in San Saba named their baby girl Diane—so I changed the baby's name to Anita Jo.

Anita Jo arrived on August 7, 1951. As Daddy and I were looking at her through the window of the nursery, Daddy asked, "Do you remember the Golden Book story, Big Toot and Little Toot?

"Uh-huh."

"Well, you'll be 'Big Toot' and the baby will be 'Little Toot,' just like the trains."

Little Toot, or "Tooter," as we came to call her, was "my" baby— just as my parents promised. I quickly learned to change her diapers, even the dirty ones. I loved to take care of her. When she cried, I tried to be the one to help her. "Look, she takes such good care of her little sister," the adults praised. I needed that attention, and even a smelly diaper could be endured to get it.

After I finished first grade, we moved to Goldthwaite, Texas; an even smaller town, twenty-two miles from San Saba. Daddy had a new job as a route man for Mrs. Baird's Bread—a step up from being a grocery check-out clerk.

The time came for that inevitable childhood request: "Daddy, I want a bicycle."

"We can't afford one right now, baby. We don't have enough money."

I wasn't happy. I wanted a bike! They had to get one for me!

Weeks later, Daddy came home and said to me, "Sister, go sweep out the back of the bread truck for me."

When I opened the door, there was a twenty-six-inch girl's bicycle; an honest-to-goodness big bicycle—my heart's desire! "Oh, Daddy, thank you! Help me get it out of the truck. Let me ride it!"

Like the swing set, my bicycle had to be bigger and better than anyone else's. I nearly crashed a dozen times trying to master it, but I got a lot of praise when I did ride my bike. And the praise made all the pain worthwhile.

In the second grade I represented my class in the annual bathing beauty contest. "We're going to get you a new bathing suit," Mother excitedly announced. She made me try on every bathing suit in the store.

"I want the red one with ruffles on the bottom," I insisted.

"Okay, we'll buy the red one."

On the day of the contest, she curled my hair perfectly, powdered my nose, and blushed my cheeks. But I got the shock of my life when the judges picked someone else as the winner! Little Carol Nan was certainly not accustomed to losing the spotlight to someone else.

Goldthwaite was a strange new place, and I felt alone and isolated. I felt as if no one cared about me. I didn't dare cry when it would be noticed, but I remember crying a lot in secret, and spending a lot of time by myself.

It's My Responsibility to Make Things Right

Life must have been pretty dull in Goldthwaite, because we went to the drive-in movie whenever a new picture came to town. We always parked beside a woman with two boys whose husband traveled all the time. She was very friendly.

"You're having an affair with that woman, aren't you?" Mother would say to Daddy. Mother constantly screamed at Daddy about this woman, but he always denied her suspicions.

I tried to intercede between them when they fought, using every weapon I could muster. Following an appendectomy, whenever they started to argue, I would bend over as though I were in excruciating pain. "My side is hurting! Stop fighting," I screamed.

"Your side is not hurting," Daddy replied. "I know what you're trying to do."

By the third grade, things had picked up for me in Goldthwaite. Butch Schuman and I were elected to represent our class in the homecoming court. When Butch shyly asked, "Carol Nan, can we go to homecoming together?" I wholeheartedly agreed.

Excitedly, I dressed in my little formal and waited for Butch to arrive. His parents came to the door with him and met my parents.

Handing me a corsage, Butch said, "You sure look pretty in that dress."

"Thank you."

We were off for a night of royalty and the applause of the crowd. For me, it was a night in heaven.

Daddy and Shorty Schuman (Butch's dad) became friends and went into the trucking business together, with plans to make a lot of money. Butch and I became playmates.

Butch's older sister, Tootie, sometimes took us swimming. She sunbathed by the deep end, where the teenage boys were. But she sternly restricted us.

"You two stay in the shallow water and keep away from me." We loved it.

Daddy's new business required him to travel with the road construction crews, providing the water trucks used in highway construction. Mother, Tooter, and I were frequently home alone at night. We all slept together in the same bed—safety in numbers, I suppose.

One night, someone tried to break in our front door.

Mother frantically shook me. "Carol Nan. Wake up! Wake up! Shhhhh. Do you hear that? What is it? Is someone trying to get in the front door?"

My heart began to race. *What should I do? Someone's trying to get in.*

"I've got to get help. Hold your sister while I call the neighbor," Mother whispered.

Hearing the activity in our house and seeing the lights come on at our next-door neighbor's, the prowler ran away.

I'll never forget the feeling of responsibility for my mother and sister that night during Daddy's absence. I was only nine.

Things were not easy for our family during those start-up years in the trucking business. Soon, however, we moved back to San Saba, into our old duplex, so Mother could go to work as a telephone operator.

Granny Gage was there to take care of Tooter and me. She made clothes for us out of scraps from Daddy's old uniforms. It was good for me; she was a fantastic cook and taught me a lot of what she knew. She also told me stories as long as I would listen—mostly stories about her years as a midwife delivering babies.

"Carol Nan, I remember when babies tried to go up instead of down. Using safety pins I'd pin a towsack around those women, just above the baby, and gradually push that baby out. You know, I delivered half of the babies in San Saba," she told me proudly. I could listen for hours.

Mother resented Granny even more by now, and said nasty things about her. But it didn't matter. I loved my Granny Gage, and I knew she loved me. Mother could say whatever she liked.

I assumed responsibility for keeping the house clean, taking care of Tooter, doing some of the cooking, buying the groceries. I knew Mother was angry with Daddy for making her go to work, so I thought if I could help with housework, things would be better for her. Maybe the tension would decrease.

Each day, Mother worked from 8:00 A.M. until noon, returning to work at 4:00 P.M. and staying until 8:00 P.M.

I waited each noon for her; so proud I had cleaned the house well and cooked her lunch—anything to make her happy. Usually, however, the four hours between noon and four were filled with anger and complaints.

"You only cleaned the surface dirt," she carped. "You didn't even look at the closet, except to hide something in it."

"Your daddy finally has enough clothes so I don't have to wash them on the weekends while he's here. But I still have to work to pay for that car he bought and wash and iron his clothes during the week."

Hearing this, I began to wash and iron Daddy's clothes, hoping to relieve the pressure on Mother. But it wasn't enough.

I remember clearly at 3:30 P.M. each day, just before Mother had to go back to work, she made me sit in a chair in the kitchen and listen to her tirades. "You bitch!" she screamed, "you can't do anything right. You half-clean the house. You put too much garlic in the food, and you wash the dark clothes with the white clothes. Can't you do anything right?"

I especially remember her calling me a "bitch" over and over, day after day. Perhaps I began to believe her.

Nothing I did was right. If I got recognition outside the home, she complained all the more about my work at the house. In her mind, I could not be doing things right outside the home when I was botching my chores at home so badly.

I felt worthless. I wanted affirmation and love, but I couldn't do anything right in mother's eyes. I tried everything, but she kept a running list of all the things I was doing wrong and frequently reminded me of them.

I was under intense pressure—at the ripe old age of eleven.

Pleasing Daddy

Finally, things started to improve for us financially. Daddy bought some acreage seven miles north of town. He loved that farm, and I loved the time we spent together there. He raised cattle and hogs, which meant more hard work. I worked right along beside him.

Raising animals would seem to lend itself to exposure to the miracle of birth, but Daddy never let me be there when an animal gave birth. It didn't seem fair to me. I was casually introduced to the death of animals as a two-year-old, but couldn't participate in their births— even though I was now eleven.

I grew up in a man's world. My mother idolized my father and taught me to do the same. I grew up believing all little girls worship their fathers, and that in return, their fathers are supposed to love and cherish them.

It was a source of pride to me that Daddy always brought in the first deer whenever he went hunting. He always killed more deer than anyone, regardless of the limit.

I often bragged to my cousin Nancy: "My daddy got the first deer. Your daddy hasn't killed a deer yet."

She sobbed, and I had won again. Inside, I felt so good.

Daddy also let me hunt with him. Almost every afternoon during deer season, just before dusk, he put Tooter and me in the car, and we drove slowly down the road, "hunting" deer—illegally. I played a game, trying to spot the deer first, always hoping to gain Daddy's approval.

"Daddy! Daddy! There's a deer," I'd say, pointing.

"Shhhhh! You're right, Carol Nan. That's a big buck. Be quiet and roll down the window. I'm going to put the gun over you, out the window, and look through the scope. Shhhhh. It's a twelve pointer!" he whispered.

My heart raced, thrilled by knowing I had spotted the deer first.

Bang! The sound of the gunfire echoed in my ears. The deer dropped to the ground without moving an inch.

"You got it, Daddy!" I squealed.

"Shhhhh! Now remember where he is. Help me watch for the game warden."

Casually we left the scene and made several passes to be sure the coast was clear. Convinced it was, Daddy stopped near the deer.

"Carol Nan, sit here and keep watch. Don't honk if you see anything. I'm going to bring the deer up to the road, and I'll be watching, too."

I sat there, breathlessly watching, loving the game I was helping Daddy play.

He jumped out of the car, hurried toward the deer, and dragged it to the side of the road. I was always relieved when I heard Daddy near the car again.

We made another pass to be sure it was still safe. When Daddy stopped this time, he opened the trunk, threw the deer inside, and we took off.

Relief! We hadn't been caught. What an exciting adventure for me with Daddy. He made some incredible shots, once killing a thirteen-point deer at over three hundred feet, a trophy deer. We ate venison year-round.

And what was this teaching me? I was learning to win at all costs—regardless of the rules.

Sometimes Daddy brought home some of the water trucks used in his business, parked them in the back yard, and cleaned them. I was so glad to see him, so eager to prove myself to him, that I worked hard cleaning those trucks.

"Sister, you're small enough to get inside those tanks," he directed. "Get in there and clean them out. Take this flashlight and go all the way back to the third compartment, and get all the black stuff out."

I was scared inside those dark tanks, but I did it anyway—to please him.

Working inside the tank, I could often hear Tooter outside, playing around Daddy. I always knew Tooter was Mother's favorite, but I wondered: Was she Daddy's favorite, too? Why shouldn't she be? She was really cute, and by now she was acting cute. I, on the other hand, felt so awkward, just as most eleven-year-old girls do. I began to feel rejected, unloved—the family Cinderella.

Jealousy began to push its way deep into my heart, as it had into my mother's. But my jealousy was directed at Little Toot. I tried to act independent, grown up—hoping to hide the hurt I was feeling. My mother and daddy seemed to have no idea of the struggle going on inside me. Daddy never knew how to express affection, to give me the affirmation I needed. Or maybe my act was just that convincing.

The glow began to leave my cheeks, the sparkle to diminish in my eyes. Working alongside my daddy, just like a man, my appreciation for gentle, soft femininity diminished. Daddy's silence was easy to accept, especially by contrast to Mother's constant complaining, which made me feel like a failure.

I helped Daddy with the farm chores, then went home and helped Mother clean the house, cook, and iron. Working with my mother, and being forced to listen to her constant moaning and complaints, I firmly resolved not to be a weak, whining woman.

I patterned my life after my father rather than my mother. Watching and listening to Daddy, my feelings and attitudes about women were badly skewed. A picture solidified in my young mind of women as total failures, weak and teary-eyed. Two guiding perceptions were formed in my imagination: My father was ultra successful and in control; my mother was a miserable drudge and out of control.

Daddy was always making fun of Mother. I was conditioned to identify with masculine qualities and to abhor feminine ones. After all, why would I not want to be like my daddy—smart, aggressive, controlling, competitive, hard working—the one with the money? Mother couldn't handle the pressure. I learned well what not to become.

My father and mother didn't realize what I was learning from them. The process began innocently, while I was a child. But with each insult to my mother, Daddy helped me bury a little more of my womanliness. I lost touch with how to be a little girl as I observed my father.

Naturally, Mother and I drifted farther and farther apart. We competed for Daddy's attention, his affection and, ultimately, his praise.

The only arena where my mother did not compete with me was in the bedroom.

How does it happen? How did a little blonde-haired, green-eyed beauty, the apple of her daddy's eye, suddenly grow out-of-date and out of fashion? How many young girls like myself, enjoying so much attention in their first years, suddenly feel they no longer deserve the hugs and kisses they once received from their father?

I loved my daddy. He was my idol and I needed his attention, but I couldn't tell him that. How many young girls face this same fate—the loss of their father's involvement in their life? I know it was unintentional, but the effects were devastating, nonetheless.

How did a little baby girl so prized by her mother when she was born become her mother's mortal enemy? I never wanted to fight with my mother. I wanted to love her and be loved by her.

How much did the evenings spent at the slaughterhouse desensitize my feelings about blood and death?

And how did `Big Toot' become so jealous of `Little Toot' in five short years?

I had begun life with a name inspired by a song. Born at Christmas time, my father chose Carol as the perfect appellation for his baby girl. But the joyous song was now hopelessly overshadowed by the strength, unalloyed by "womanly" weakness that I had come to value to the exclusion of all else. Where would it lead?

3

....

THE POWER OF SEX

GROWING UP isn't easy. Puberty came, and I developed quickly and abundantly.

My thirteenth birthday, one of our first boy-girl parties, was celebrated at the home of my friend, Cheri Mays. I was the center of attention as thirty kids gathered around the cake to sing "Happy Birthday."

"Happy Birthday to you. Happy Birthday to you. Happy Birthday, Car-ol Na-an…"

But carrying over all the other voices, Dwight sang, "Happy Birthday, dear 'Chesty'…"

Embarrassed and humiliated, I ran out of the room crying.

I had done everything to play down my new shape. In spite of my efforts, growth continued, along with relentless and open teasing. The boys even accused me of wearing "falsies." It's a wonder my spine isn't deformed from years of slumping over, trying not to show.

The living conditions at home made it even worse. Our single-bedroom duplex afforded little privacy for a family of four.

I hated the situation. All four of us slept in one bedroom, which contained two double beds. I didn't want to be in the same room with my parents at night. I was too old to be there. "Let me sleep downstairs," I begged. "I want to sleep in a room alone."

"You don't need to be downstairs, Carol Nan. We wouldn't be able to hear you if you needed us." Mother's fearful nature once again rose to the surface.

I complained until, finally, they let me. But whenever I acted up—which, for a girl of thirteen, was often enough—my punishment was the loss of my downstairs sleeping privilege.

I will always remember the sounds of their lovemaking at night. I hated it. One night I covered my ears, trying to stop the sound—but I couldn't. "Stop it!" I finally screamed.

Daddy jumped on top of me. "Shut up!" he screamed, as he beat me through the covers. It really hurt, but I kept quiet.

They never made me sleep upstairs again.

I still was responsible to take care of Tooter most of the time. As a result, she had to go everywhere I did. Of course, I blamed Mother for not taking care of her as she was supposed to. Being crowded into a three-room duplex was tough, but having my seven-year-old sister along with me everywhere I went was too much.

I longed for freedom with my friends, and complained to my parents. "No one else has to take their little sister with them. Can't Tooter stay with someone else? Why do I always have to take her with me?"

"Tooter doesn't bother you and your friends. It doesn't hurt you to take her with you," Mother usually answered.

"I'm the only person I know who has to take care of her little sister! I hate it."

They refused to listen and warned, "Carol Nan, you better take care of Tooter and treat her right." But they never told Tooter to obey me. I felt violated and helpless.

Tooter probably longed to be my age. She tried to talk and act like my older friends, but I believe she needed to be with children her own age. She was forced to be older than she was ready to be.

Unbelievably, my first dating experiences were not hampered by Tooter's presence. The boy's family would come to the house, drop us off at whatever event we were attending, pick us up again, and then deliver me back home.

Whenever we went to a Baptist youth- group party where dancing was forbidden, we would lock out the chaperones and start dancing anyway. I was always the ringleader.

"Turn up the record player. They can't get in until we unlock the door!"

"If we slow-dance, they'll get upset. Let's jitterbug."

"Look, they're outside knocking on the window. What are we going to do?"

"Keep dancing," I'd say. "They'll think we don't hear them."

Given the way most Baptists feel about dancing, it was inevitable that I would attend the Methodist Church.

I guess Mother wasn't a good Baptist either, because dancing brought her to life and even improved our relationship. She was more than happy to teach me and my friends (especially the Baptist ones) to dance.

I had a lot of close friends—Mary Lou, Cheri, Jo, Jonibeth, Kay, Brenda, Nancy, Terry, Margaret, Sylvia, Loy Nell, Karen. We did everything together. Our house was small and we couldn't have parties there, but Mother chauffeured us everywhere to try and make up for it. Those were the "good ole days"!

Early Conquests

I was a young teenager, and the boys were giving me lots of attention. The nicknames, and the awkwardness of my early physical development had faded away. Older boys noticed me now. I was on center stage again, and I loved the recognition. What I had lost from my daddy, I found in young men—most older than me.

In the seventh and eighth grades, I met boys at the movies. I had several boyfriends, always the popular boys. I especially liked Franklin, but Mother didn't approve. Dwight and I talked so much on the phone that Daddy called him the "telephone kid." I started going steady with him.

Dwight was popular and handsome; he was blonde—and tall enough to be a good dancer. We learned how to dance together, even the jitterbug.

Most of the boys were too shy to learn to jitterbug, but Dwight had a lot of self-confidence. He had learned to dance from my mother, along with a number of my other friends. It wasn't any time at all before he knew all the steps.

"Come on, Carol Nan. Let's dance," he would urge.

I loved to dance with Dwight.

Dwight was special to me for another reason, too; he was the first boy I ever kissed. It happened on my first hay ride; I was so thrilled. Even though we met the boys at the hay ride, everyone had a "date" and Dwight was mine.

We rode the entire evening under our blankets, many of the girls hoping they would be kissed for the first time. Sitting cramped between other couples, we talked through our blankets. At the end of the evening, as we approached the town, the hay wagon became very quiet.

An eternity of silence later, Dwight put his arms around me, pulled me close, and kissed me on the lips.

"Wow!" Dwight said, afterward.

Wow! I thought. *This is neat!*

I was learning to compete for boys. It was great fun. The more unavailable they were, the more my competitive instincts were aroused.

My friend Cheri was always talking about an older boy named John Richardson. "John works for my dad at the feed store. He is so cute! I would love to go out with him, but my parents wouldn't let me even if he asked," she pined. "They think he's too old for me."

My parents felt the same way about John, but he was the best-looking boy I'd ever seen. I thought he was gorgeous. He was dark-complexioned, with auburn hair and brown eyes. He was at least six feet tall. Every girl in high school wanted to date John—especially some of my girlfriends. Their folks wouldn't allow them to go out with him, but I knew I could manipulate *my* parents.

Like my daddy, cruising the fence-rows for deer, I was on a hunt. He always came in first, so I wanted to be first, too. So what if the rules had to be bent a little? What difference did it make, as long as I didn't get caught? I was willing to do whatever was necessary to get what I wanted—and I wanted John because he was untouchable. What would it take to claim him? What would be the cost to win this contest?

At the end of the summer, just before I was to start high school, John called.

"Carol Nan, this is John Richardson. Would you go to the drive-in with me Friday night?"

"Yes, I'd love to! What time will you pick me up?"

"Seven-thirty."

"I'll be ready."

John was a senior; I was fourteen. He was supposed to be out of reach—which made him instantly desirable. When I was younger, I always felt inadequate, especially around popular boys. I hated that feeling then and determined to change it. When John asked me out, I knew I had accomplished my first goal. Awkwardness had been replaced by excitement—the allure of the unknown.

By this time, the chasm between my father and me had become so wide that I wasn't concerned about what he thought. In fact, I wanted to date John, just to show Daddy I could. John reminded me of my father in so many ways. Looking back, it seems obvious that he was taking my daddy's place, giving me the attention I was not getting from my father. At the time, though, all I knew was that I was determined to go out with John Richardson—despite what my parents might think.

When I started dating John, things at home were stormy. Mother was very unhappy, complaining constantly about Daddy. After he had been home one weekend, Mother confided in me.

"Your father slept with another woman."

"He—what? Who would Daddy sleep with?"

"Some woman he picked up on a trip."

"How did you find out?"

"He told me."

"You mean he confessed?"

"Yes. He feels guilty about it."

"You don't have anything to worry about then. It won't happen again."

But Mother didn't agree with me. "I'm thinking about divorcing him," she declared.

I pondered the secret she had shared with me. *Mother is building her case, preparing for divorce. Why is she so upset? What difference does it make that Daddy had sex with another woman? After all—he came home to Mother, as usual.*

I chalked another demerit beside Mother's name on the invisible slate I kept in my mind. It made no difference to me that she had confided in me about Daddy's transgression. Couldn't she see that my role model could do no wrong in my eyes? He set his own rules, as he always had. And so did I. My only curfews were self-imposed; my parents continued their unrestricted ways with me, as they had since I was born.

John cared a lot about me—or so it seemed. The more time we spent together, the more volatile our physical attraction became. He seemed much more experienced than I; it appeared he had played around a lot.

After months of dating, he made his move. "When are you going to loosen up, Carol Nan?" he asked.

"What do you mean?"

"We've been dating for some time, but you won't even let me unbutton your blouse. Why don't you relax a little?" he drawled.

"John, I'm scared."

"Trust me, Carol Nan," he said in a tone that wasn't quite a request.

It was quite clear that we were either going to be more intimate, or he was going to drop me. I didn't want that! I now knew the price tag for keeping John.

It was time to compromise; time to bend the rules.

I wanted John for the prestige our relationship conferred on me. I understood his reputation was not good, but I didn't care. He wanted me. The exchange would give both of us what we wanted.

At about eleven o'clock on a cold night, parked on top of Chapel Hill, in the back seat of John's car, I did what I thought was necessary to keep him. I was nervous, but ready for all those wonderful, explosive things that are supposed to happen at your first sexual encounter.

Control by Manipulation

My expectations of bliss and special bonding with John were short-lived, but the pain seemed endless. John seemed oblivious to my suffering. Where was the ecstasy? Where was the pleasure? This was hard, cold pain—nothing more.

I controlled my emotions outwardly that evening, but, once alone, I grieved over the loss of that one thing a girl reserves for her special troubadour—the gift she can give but once. I surrendered my innocence that night, but I had also learned how to use my physical and emotional resources to manipulate people, especially men, to get what I wanted.

John felt more guilty than I did. The next day he was remorseful.

"Carol Nan, let's just forget that last night ever happened."

"How can I forget last night?" *The damage is done,* I thought. *Now he wants to walk away. Well, he won't get off the hook that easily!*

"I'm sorry for pushing you into having sex with me," he said. Oh, so that was it! He felt he had wronged me, without knowing I had used him, too. We were both used, but I was the only one who fully understood, who consented to the exploitation.

I now suspected that last night was also the first time for John, and I saw a weakness—a weakness I could bend to my advantage. I knew John enjoyed our sexual encounter, and I was going to be sure there were more, no matter how painful it was for me.

I saw something more. I could also use his sense of guilt to control him. If we continued to have sex, he would feel obligated to stay with me. This was the first time I realized what a powerful lever sex can be. I knew I could control John with sex—and I did, for two-and-a-half years.

But the sword cuts both ways. Once at a party with our friends, John grabbed me. "Carol Nan, you were flirting with Charlie," he accused. "You'd better straighten up."

"I wasn't flirting with Charlie or anyone else," I responded.

"Yes, you were!" he said angrily, and he slapped me.

His jealousy was too much, along with the physical abuse and embarrassment. A lot of other boys wanted to date me; I didn't need John anymore. I broke it off with him.

I was sixteen. A boy named Mike invited me to homecoming. Jim Bob Everett was there. Mike and I danced a few times; then Jim Bob approached me. "Carol Nan, would you like to dance?"

"I'd love to, Jim Bob." We glided out on the floor. I was determined to impress Jim Bob, a college man enrolled at Southwest Texas State.

"How's college?" I asked.

"Fine. I like San Marcos."

"What's your major?"

"Pharmacy, but I'll have to transfer to the University of Texas to finish my degree. What are you doing tomorrow night?"

"Nothing."

"Would you like to go to the drive-in with me?"

"Sure."

"I'll pick you up at seven."

Jim Bob was a far better catch than John Richardson. He had graduated from high school fourth in his class, was a member of the National Honor Society, captain of the football team, and very popular.

Jim Bob and I continued dancing throughout the evening. Mike pretended not to notice. At the end of the dance, Mike took me home and never asked me out again. I don't think I gave it a second thought.

Jim Bob and I started dating immediately. Here I was, at age sixteen, dating a very popular guy. And I was doing all right in the popularity arena myself—that December I was selected as a princess in the local Pecan Queen contest.

Daddy was out of town on business at the time of the contest, but got home before we did. "How did you do?" he called as Mother and I walked in the door after it was over.

"I'm a Pecan Princess."

"That's great for your first entry. You'll be the Queen next year!" I beamed with pride.

And Then It Happened

Jim Bob and I made a cute couple. Even Jim Bob's mother, Catherine, was proud of her son for dating a Pecan Princess. "I heard you were beautiful at the Pecan Queen contest. Congratulations. I'm proud of you," Catherine Everett said with a smile.

Jim Bob enjoyed necking, but he always stopped short of anything else. But once I helped him unbutton my dress, he caught on quickly. I went back to what I knew—using sex to control a relationship. Soon we were having intercourse every weekend.

"Are you sure you won't get pregnant now?" he once asked me, worriedly.

"This is supposed to be a safe time," I assured him. He didn't need much more persuasion.

We had been dating for three months in late December 1961 when I first suspected I was pregnant—just two-and-a-half weeks after being named a Pecan Princess.

What a turn of events! This was certainly not the kind of attention I was looking for.

I was scared. Would Jim Bob believe the baby was his? Almost paralyzed by the fear of rejection, I told him. "Jim Bob, I've missed my period. I think I'm pregnant."

"How do we find out for sure?"

"I can go to the doctor in Goldthwaite. No one will see me there."

"When can you go?"

"Saturday."

He struggled with the news, especially since others were telling him that I was still seeing John—which wasn't true. He finally believed me about that, at least.

Quite a dilemma: A sixteen-year-old girl, living in a small town, popular in high school, holding a student body office—what does she do when she thinks she's pregnant?

I had no idea how to proceed. I was scared, but I was excited, too, in a strange way. The thought that I could have a baby was unbelievable. And I could feel my body making changes. I was going to be a mother! I think even Jim Bob was excited.

Since Jim Bob was home for Christmas, I took his car and some money, dressed in adult clothes, and went to the doctor in Goldthwaite. I borrowed eyeglasses and changed my appearance as much as I could, hoping no one would recognize me there.

I checked in at Dr. Childress's office under the name of Sonia Sears, telling him I was sixteen and married. As proof, I wore a pearl ring that John had given me, turning the pearl underneath to make the ring look like a wedding band.

I was thrilled with the news of my pregnancy. Dr. Childress, a kind man, asked if I needed any help. I said, "No, everything is all right."

I rushed back to San Saba to tell Jim Bob. "I'm pregnant! The baby will be born in August!" I exclaimed.

"We'll get married right away," he assured me.

"I love you, Jim Bob."

"I love you, too."

When he said we'd get married, I was really relieved. We had talked about marriage before, but not under these circumstances.

Now we had to face our parents. Jim Bob didn't mind telling his folks, but I feared telling mine. I couldn't stand the thought of the punishment I expected, nor the withdrawal of love and approval I knew I faced. I decided simply to tell my parents we wanted to get married at semester break—without mentioning my pregnancy.

Jim Bob was lucky. Deer season was on, and Sam, his father, was out in the middle of nowhere at a deer camp. So he told his mother first. She was upset, but handled it well. We then drove to the camp together and told his father.

"Welcome to the family, Carolyn Ann," Sam said, before giving me a kiss. He never got my name right, but I loved him anyway, because he was so sweet.

He was encouraging then, but his tune changed when he got back home to his wife. By this time Catherine determined that her "Jim Bobby" was being trapped into marriage, and she blamed me for the pregnancy. Perhaps she sensed what only another woman could.

I don't know to this day how Jim Bob stood up to his mother. I guess he really loved me.

I could not and did not tell my parents the truth. Mother had always stressed how important my virginity was. "Don't have sex before you're married," she warned. "Remember, you're like a rosebud. If you force a rosebud open too early, it's ugly. If you let it open naturally, in its own time, it's beautiful."

"Good" girls didn't get pregnant—only girls who weren't smart enough to avoid it. As I had planned, I told my parents only part of the truth. "Jim Bob and I are going to get married between semesters in January."

"You can't get married! You're too young. I won't sign for you!" my mother screamed.

"Married? If you're that stupid, *I'll* sign for you." My father helped me without even realizing what he had done. I didn't have to tell them the truth. I was relieved beyond words.

"Why do you want to get married? Are you pregnant?" Mother later quizzed.

"No. I'm not pregnant. Jim Bob and I love each other. We've just decided that we don't want to wait."

"You have your whole life ahead of you. This is such a mistake."

I thought, *If you only knew how much I don't want to get married now. I don't have a choice.*

As the wedding date drew near, Scott Benson, the president of the Student Council and a dear friend, came to see me. As a sophomore, I had been nominated for president of the Student Council. In my junior year I was elected to the Student Council and served as secretary. Scott was certain I would be elected president in my senior year.

"Carol Nan, you ought to reconsider getting married," he said. "You're throwing away some honors in your senior year that will look good later." Then he asked me, point-blank, "Are you pregnant?"

Of course I denied it. At that time, how dearly I wished the only thing I had to worry about was being elected president of the Student Council my senior year—rather than becoming a mother.

To say I had mixed emotions about getting married would be quite an understatement. Although the prospect was thrilling, this was such a final step out of a world I was not ready to leave. By my own manipulation I had prematurely enlarged my boundaries into an adult world with adult responsibilities. I saw Jim Bob as a way of escape from all the griping, complaining, and condescension at home. But now my options were severely limited.

Still, even at the last minute, I would have backed out if I hadn't been pregnant.

Strangely, I even worried about letting my parents down. In the back of my mind I thought, *Who is going to be there to help Mother cook and clean the house?* What a thing to be thinking about! My home, as bad as it had seemed to me, was more attractive at this moment than I ever dreamed it could be.

Rules are made to be broken, aren't they? But I didn't realize the high cost to be paid when one gets caught. And Jim Bob and I were just beginning to pay for our mistake.

4

....

FOR BETTER
OR FOR WORSE

M Y NAME CHANGED from Carol Nan Gage to Carol Nan
Everett on Friday, January 26, 1962. For better or for worse, Jim
Bob had a strong young woman on his hands, one who needed a lot of
attention and a firm hand to rein her in. Only time would tell if he
could do it.

We were married at the First Baptist Church in San Saba with only
our families and close friends present. As we drove to Austin later that
night for our honeymoon, I asked, "Jim Bob, where are we going to
stay tonight?"

"I thought we would find a cheap motel on the expressway."

"How much can we afford?"

"We need to find as cheap a room as possible."

I spotted a nice motel that I wanted to stay in, but Jim Bob said,
"Let's go to the one next door. It looks cheaper."

We drove in. Jim Bob registered us, and came back dangling a
room key from his hand. "Only six dollars for the night!" he exclaimed.

The marriage had started.

On Saturday morning, my parents helped us move into the married student housing at the University of Texas at Austin—"student
housing" consisted of six hundred old army barracks from World War
II which had been converted into apartments.

Daddy was not happy with our first home. "Is this where my
daughter is going to live?" he asked Jim Bob skeptically.

"Yes. We'll only pay twenty-eight dollars per month plus half of
our electricity," Jim Bob replied. "This is all we can afford, but we'll be
around a lot of other married students here. We'll move to a nicer place
as soon as we can afford it," Jim Bob explained.

"Well, this looks like a cedar chopper's village. I can't believe you're going to live here," Daddy said to me, in a voice loud enough for Jim Bob to hear.

Believe it or not, I really loved my new home. We received so many shower gifts that we didn't need anything to be ready for housekeeping except a broom—and my parents supplied a nice one. It was fun having my own home, and I enjoyed the feeling of independence.

The Monday morning after our wedding, Jim Bob started the spring semester at the University of Texas and I enrolled in Austin High School to finish my junior year. I took six courses that semester and two more by correspondence. I graduated from high school without having to attend during my senior year.

We went to school all week, studied at night, and on the weekends rushed home to San Saba. We both felt guilty about what we had done to our parents. To atone, Jim Bob worked at his father's service station while I cleaned my parents' house. I also got our clothes clean for the next week.

My parents gave us twenty dollars a week and gasoline credit cards. Jim Bob's father gave us one hundred and fifty dollars a month—the same amount he had been giving him before our marriage. I don't remember lacking for anything. We actually seemed to have more than enough money for our needs.

At times during those first months, I was very sick; I sometimes worried about losing the baby. The thought that a person was growing in me was exciting, and I never doubted it was going to be a boy.

I was seventeen, newly married, and pregnant. Today the world would say to such a young woman, "You can do anything you want— except have a baby in a crisis situation." Thank God I didn't hear those voices then. Abortion was unthinkable at that time.

Aborting a child violates everything a woman's normally-functioning body wants to do and is supposed to do. I was alive. A baby boy was alive inside me. Sure, it was tough. Yes, I was sick. Certainly, finishing school was difficult—but it was all worth it.

Old Problems Resurface

We had been married two months when I first felt rejection from Jim Bob. Like my mother's experience as a young bride, I came to believe Jim Bob preferred his mother over me. And I wanted to have first place in my husband's life.

One Sunday afternoon, while returning to Austin, we argued. It had been a rough weekend for me, and I couldn't understand Jim Bob's casual attitude about the things that disturbed me. "Your mother is so nasty to me," I said. "There's no one in the world that can get along with her. I do everything I can to help her, and she still hates me," I said with a pout.

"My mother doesn't hate you," he insisted.

"Yes, she does. She blames me for forcing you into marriage. Well, I didn't do this by myself." The old martyr routine—I played it to the hilt.

"You'll just have to overlook my mother for a while."

I couldn't believe what I heard. "Overlook your mother? What about me? Why don't you make her be nice to me, instead of making me overlook her?" I demanded.

"You overlook my mother," Jim Bob threatened, "or I'll take you back to your parents and leave you. I mean it! Now shut up about it."

I was crushed! It seemed Jim Bob loved his mother more than me and I couldn't express my feelings on the subject unless I wanted to be alone and pregnant. I felt stifled, stomped on.

That very day I began building a case against my husband and his mother. I would get back at him for rejecting me and at her for being the apparent reason. I was intimately acquainted with rejection from my growing-up years; now rejection had entered my marriage. I was devastated! I never expected this from Jim Bob, never dreamed he would choose his mother over me.

Jealousy had now poisoned my heart toward my husband and mother-in-law. I was reliving the nightmare my mother had endured before me.

Today, I realize I was wrong. I was not rejected as a child nearly as much as I believed; but I chose to believe a lie. And in the early stages of my marriage to Jim Bob, as well as in most other relationships, I continued to believe that lie.

As a result, I chose to retaliate, to follow destructive paths that assured my rejection for many years. Throughout my life, I have done more than enough to destroy many potentially wholesome relationships or to run away from them.

Before we married—and before I became pregnant—I dreamed we would have a huge home with a large master bedroom. In the bedroom would be a window overlooking pastures full of cattle on our ranch. We would have three or four children. I would be able to wear expensive clothes and we would be members of the upper tier of San Saba society. That was my dream—but now it was so far from reality that I couldn't appreciate what I did have.

Our marriage came to seem irrelevant. I knew of no happily married couples. Everyone seemed to be discontented, fighting all the time, or having affairs. I had always thought the way to keep a man happy was to please him sexually. I decided to make certain I did that, even if it seemed mundane to me.

Joe Bob, our first child, was born September 12, 1962. He was truly here—my baby! The struggles I had endured faded beside the joy of holding our son. I really hoped the birth of a child would finally make us a family—and, for a while at least, we made a promising start.

We put a lot of energy into Joe Bob because we both were crazy about him. He slept with us. Both sets of grandparents lavished affection on him. He was sick a lot, which only gave me more reason to hold him.

But the euphoria of a new life soon wore off. Soon it was back to my old ways, back to the "war zone" with the Everett family. Now, however, there was another reason to fight with them and another weapon to use against them—my son.

Joe Bob was only five months old when his ten-month-old cousin bit him. At the time, we were driving around Austin with the in-laws of Jim Bob's brother. As I comforted the sobbing Joe Bob, I said, in everyone's hearing, "That's okay, Joe Bob. In a few months you'll be old enough to bite Devin!"

Neither Billy Don nor Pat apologized for their son biting mine. They just silently got out of our car when we returned home, and left. Soon the whole Everett family knew how "hateful" I'd been.

I wanted Jim Bob to say something to them, but he wanted peace at all costs. He actually told me to be quiet. "Just be nice around my family. It sure wouldn't hurt if you at least tried to be *quiet* around them."

I felt he was choosing them over us. I couldn't believe he wouldn't take up for his own child.

As soon as I finished high school, I enrolled in business college. My plan was to prepare for a job so we could stop taking money from Jim

Bob's parents. Then we wouldn't have to go back to San Saba so often. But before I finished business college, I was pregnant again.

Our daughter, Kelly Kay, was born on August 27, 1964. We moved out of the married student housing into low-income housing to get more space. How I wanted us to be the perfect American family! We certainly had a good start—a firstborn son and a beautiful daughter.

I actually thought of Kelly as a sort of live doll. I wanted to dress her up in ruffles and keep her that way. I dressed her in very girlish, lacy clothes until she started walking; then I started buying matching outfits for her and her brother.

Joe Bob was very proud of his little sister, and he really tried to take care of her. Of course, at two years of age his care was questionable: He would help her eat her ice cream by stuffing the cone in her face, getting it all over her. Despite such episodes, Kelly loved her brother; they played together all the time, with surprisingly few arguments.

Catherine Everett and I had ceased speaking to each other by this time. Even I knew that had to change. Things were so strained between us that Jim Bob could not even ask his family to visit us. I finally extended an invitation for them to come to our home, hoping to help matters. It did, and we slowly began to rebuild our relationship. Sad to say, it was only a short term fix.

The Battle for Control Rages

Our marriage had much potential, but I did my best to destroy it. We both started out with the same goal in life: Jim Bob wanted what I wanted, a loving family. We just couldn't make it work.

In my eyes, Jim Bob grew weaker with each passing year. He failed some of his courses and spent time with his friends, drinking and gambling. Sometimes he lost as much as two hundred dollars at a time in poker games; we had to borrow money to pay the gambling bills. Things were becoming unbearable.

Seven months after Kelly Kay was born, I went to work as a secretary in an insurance company. I did well and was promoted. Jim Bob continued to party with his friends, to the detriment of his grades.

In the fourth year of our marriage, we had a big argument one evening. I'd had enough of his lifestyle, and he was sick of my working all the time.

"Why don't you ever come home?" I demanded. "You're either at school, at work, out drinking with your friends, or playing poker. You never spend any time with me and the kids."

"I need some time to relax," he answered.

"Why not relax with us?" I countered. "I need to relax, too. It's not relaxing at all for me when you're out drinking until all hours of the night. And another thing—every time you're playing poker, I wonder how much money I've lost. You never bring the money home to me when you win, but if you lose, it's my loss too. If you have to borrow money to pay your gambling debts, I have to help pay it back."

I was worn out by now with the same old things. Would they ever improve? I didn't see how. "I just want a divorce," I said, finally. I had reached the end of my rope.

"Just stay with me until I get out of school," he said, "and then, if you still want a divorce, I'll pay to put you through college," Jim Bob promised.

But I put no stock in that promise. I began planning to divorce him that night, never dreaming it would be another three-and-a-half years before he would graduate. It took him a total of eight-and-a-half years to get his diploma. Seven of those years he was married to me. I suppose it was "our" degree.

I knew that when I divorced Jim Bob, I would have to make more money than I was now making in order to support myself and my two children. It would be my responsibility to make as much, if not more, money than their father would make when he became a pharmacist. This became my challenge. I didn't see that as a problem—only an opportunity to compete with men as I had been trained to do by my father.

I was recruited as a salesperson by Tupperware and I jumped on it. I became the youngest manager in the Southwest Region at age twenty-one, and quickly climbed into the Top Ten in sales. I received the first check for three hundred dollars written by my distributorship up until that time. I was furnished a car and had forty-two women working for me. I was rolling!

Jim Bob perceived my success as a further threat to our marriage. "Carol Nan, you need to quit Tupperware and get a day job so you can be home with me and the kids at night," he insisted.

"How will we live if I give up this good job with Tupperware? We'd have to buy a car. I can't make this kind of money anywhere in an eight-to-five job."

"I'll be getting out of school soon and I'll get a raise at the highway department," he replied. "I'll take care of it."

I quit Tupperware. I was confused—wanting to believe him, but not quite able. A part of me wanted to divorce Jim Bob, but another part still wanted the marriage to work.

I went to work—for less money—at Austin Diagnostic Clinic. This was my first, but not my last, exposure to the medical world. I started as a bookkeeper and soon became credit manager for the clinic.

Life with Jim Bob continued to get worse. The more he stayed away and did poorly in college, the more we fought and the greater was my desire to strike back at him. I tried to warn him, to get his attention. I punished him every way I could think of for neglecting me and the children. Nothing changed in his life; I was so frustrated that I used every weapon I had.

I stopped keeping the house clean, especially washing the dishes. He just bought a dishwasher. The poor guy certainly wasn't a mind reader, but how could he be so blind? Didn't he realize that I needed him—not appliances?

Getting Even... and Getting Free

Early in the sixth year of our marriage, I began to think of having an affair. If I did, it would be someone close to Jim Bob, in order to hurt him—just as he had hurt me.

Once the idea germinated, it became very appealing to me. I could set my own boundaries—and besides, the hunt would be fun. I had been free to make up my own rules all my life; no boundaries had ever been set for me. Why should it be any different now?

My mother had called me a bitch. Since being nice to Jim Bob was not working, I reasoned, it was time to change the rules—to see if he would respond differently. Of course, I didn't consider myself a bitch, only a strong woman doing what she must do to get her husband to do what she wants. I didn't believe I was doing anything terribly wrong.

I had watched Daddy treat Mother similarly. His extramarital affair had gotten a response from her. Maybe an affair would work similarly with Jim Bob.

I picked my first target—the right time, place, and the perfect prey.

The affair went on for the remainder of our marriage. I soon picked other targets. Each time Jim Bob and I fought or he stayed out late, I had someone waiting to spend time with me who would give me the attention I wanted. And so I continued, playing a destructive game to punish a "weak" husband.

In the early spring of 1969, Jim Bob tried to act responsibly, to become a real husband and provider. He was close to graduation, and I suppose he wanted to prove his readiness for the real world. But he went about it the wrong way.

I had worked very hard to help us get ahead. We had been able to buy a house because of my job at the clinic. Suddenly, without telling me, he closed all our charge accounts.

I stormed into the house and confronted him. "I went to the French Bootery today to buy some shoes. They wouldn't let me charge! They pulled my account, and it had a note on it that said, 'Account closed at husband's request.' Do you have any idea how embarrassing that was? If you were going to close my account, the very least you could have done is told me so I wouldn't have tried to charge."

"I knew you'd be mad," he said calmly.

"Didn't you think I would find out?"

"Yes. I knew you would."

"I've paid that account myself for years. You had no right to close it."

"I've closed all of our charge accounts."

"Without discussing it with me?"

"Yes."

"I thought when you said you would take care of everything that you meant you'd take care of the bills. I didn't know I was going to have to cut down on buying things. Jim Bob, you have no right to treat me this way."

He wouldn't answer me. End of discussion—because he was the man, the boss. It was shades of our honeymoon again. Jim Bob hadn't learned, after six years of marriage, that I was not a cheap date. I wasn't going for that. He had no right to take charge now—not this way. I had worked to put him through school, and now he wanted me to be the weak, submissive wife and let him be the strong one in the family. No way!

It was open war. Later that night, I reminded him, "Jim Bob, you'll be through with school in August. I agreed to stay with you until you were out of school. In three months you'll be out. I want a divorce then."

"Things will be so different when I'm out of school, Carol Nan. This is no time to get a divorce." Things were going to be all better, just like that—as if I should believe his promises.

"I've lived with you too long, Jim Bob; things aren't going to be better when you're out of school." I gathered up the kids and went to San Saba for the summer. I started having fun, living a life completely apart from him.

While we were separated, he tried everything he could to get me to come back. He even said what I never expected to hear: "We'll stop going to San Saba every weekend. I'll never go back there again if you'll come back to me."

He had finally said it, finally said he would put me before his mother. But it was too late. By now, I didn't believe him or care; I was through trusting him.

Jim Bob even followed me once, when I went out on a date with an admirer. He caught us at the lake together and followed me home. I went to my parents' house. He came in and began yelling a familiar name at me: bitch.

"Kick him out of here. Get him away from me," I pleaded with my father.

"No, Carol Nan. We're not going to ask him to leave. These children belong to him, too," Daddy responded.

I turned around, facing Jim Bob angrily. "Get out of here or I'm going to kill you."

He kept calling me a bitch. I went to my father's closet to get his gun. Jim Bob left.

I filed for divorce immediately. All I wanted was out.

He promised again we would never have to go back to San Saba if I would change my mind. But seven years of rejection (as I perceived it) was too much to overcome.

In the divorce settlement, Jim Bob suffered a convenient lapse of memory.

"You promised that if I helped you get through school, you'd help me get through," I said. "I need to go to college now. I want you to help me," I reminded him.

"I never said that, Carol Nan."

I was livid, but hardly surprised. "I've taken care of you all this time. I could never depend on you before; why should I be able to depend on you now?"

Jim Bob finally signed the divorce papers when I agreed to pay my own attorney's fees. The divorce was finalized in November 1969.

I suppose Jim Bob proved too weak to handle me. Or was I too weak to face myself?

5

....

A Promise Kept...
A Life Lost

MY DIVORCE ATTORNEY gave me some free advice when my divorce became final. "Consider yourself a rabbit in a large carrot patch. Be selective; you don't have to take the first carrot you see," he said.

I was a twenty-four-year-old, newly emancipated bunny in a whole patch of big, juicy carrots. There I was, in Austin, Texas, with thousands of handsome young male university students. It was the end of the sixties, when "Free Love" was the watchword of the day.

I knew what men wanted and how to control them: Sex was the weapon I would use to get what I wanted. I believed all men were fundamentally weak, desiring only sexual gratification and not caring about the whole person.

Whenever I did chance to meet a man with real strength, I didn't stay around long—because I knew he couldn't be controlled. He might want a "stay-at-home" housewife and mother for his children, a part I wasn't willing to play.

Earlier, Jim Bob helped a friend get a job at the Texas Highway Department, where he had worked while he was in school. In early 1970, after our divorce, I called Jim Bob at work. The telephone line was crossed to someone else by mistake.

"Hello. This is Tom White," a strong voice answered.

I knew Tom. We had originally met when he and his first wife, Susan, lived in the married student housing unit next to ours at the University of Texas. Our families had maintained only limited contact after Jim Bob and I bought our own house and moved away.

"This is Carol, Tom—Carol Nan Everett. I was calling Jim Bob. Something must have happened," I apologized.

"I just dialed out. I guess our lines got crossed."

We had a brief conversation, and he told me he and Susan were divorced. Then he asked, "Are you busy tonight?"

"No."

"Would you meet me for a cup of coffee?" he suggested.

We met at a local restaurant and talked about our families and our lives. Then he told me that his father was dying with cancer.

Tom was more physically and intellectually attractive that evening than I had remembered. He was the fraternity man I had always wanted. But after that evening, I didn't hear from Tom again for several months.

In the meantime, I self-destructed at Austin Diagnostic Clinic. I was fired for constant lateness and for fighting a running battle with a co-worker.

I decided to go back to San Saba. I moved into the other half of my parents' duplex. Granny Gage had moved out of the duplex into her own little house across the street. It was peaceful there, and the children quickly settled in to kindergarten and first grade.

The carrot patch in San Saba was almost empty; it had been picked over quite well. The bunny rabbit was about to starve to death when Tom called from Austin.

"Carol Nan, this is Tom White. Did you move to San Saba?"

"Yes, about a month ago."

"Do you ever get back to Austin?"

"About once a week, so I can keep my sanity!"

"When are you coming back to town?"

"Tomorrow."

"How about dinner tomorrow night?"

"Great. I'll call you when I get to town to find out where to meet you." I was ecstatic! A big, juicy carrot!

Tom and I started seeing each other every weekend in Austin, and I stayed in his apartment when I was there. Early one Friday afternoon, he called to break our weekend date. "I won't be able to see you this weekend; my dad just died."

I felt so cold, sympathizing with his loss. I didn't know what to say. "I—I'm sorry about your father's death," I blurted. "When are you going to Monahans?"

"My plane leaves in about two hours."

I knew he was alone and I longed to be with him. He sounded so empty when I hung up the phone that I called him back. "I don't know what to say, but I feel so sad. I just want you to know I truly care. Is there anything I can do?"

"No. But thanks for calling. I'll call you when I get back." He seemed relieved to hear my voice.

Two weeks after the funeral, we both went to see his mother at her home in Monahans, Texas. Faye White was quite a lady—beautiful, very poised; she seemed to be adjusting gracefully to her husband's death. But I knew by the time we left her home that she didn't want her son to marry a woman with two children. I also knew I was not on the same social plane as them. In San Saba we only had two levels—those "with it" and those "not with it." In Monahans, there was another level—"the uppercrusts."

The Whites were "uppercrust."

Faye White didn't think she had to worry about a marriage between Tom and me. So, true to form, marrying Tom became a challenge I couldn't resist.

While I was seeing Tom, Daddy was planning my future in San Saba. "Baby, I've been thinking about getting you a few hogs and putting them out north of town. I think you can make a pretty good living raising hogs," he suggested one day.

My response? "Can I borrow three hundred dollars to move back to Austin?"

"Yes," he replied.

I don't know if he planned for the hogs to get rid of me, but if so it worked. I was sure Daddy wasn't aware that "uppercrusts" in Monahans look down their noses at female hog farmers from San Saba.

Married in Red

I moved back to Austin, leaving the children in San Saba until I got settled. I went to work as the credit manager at Holy Cross Hospital and moved into an apartment close to Tom's. He kept his apartment, but his clothes stayed at my place.

Tom was sexually exciting to me, and we spent most of our free time in bed. I wanted Tom to be my husband; I wanted us to live together the rest of our lives.

The time came for the children to rejoin me in Austin. Tom didn't think it was a good idea. "Carol Nan, why don't you leave the kids in San Saba with their grandparents?" he asked.

"Jim Bob will try to get custody of the kids if I do. There is no way I'm going to give him the opportunity to get my children."

When I brought them home, Tom and I continued to have the same living arrangement. But despite the fact that I liked him—perhaps loved him—I didn't like the impression my children were getting about family, about the husband/wife relationship. I gave him an ultimatum: "Either we marry or we break off the relationship," I said.

When he didn't respond, I decided to set up a date with a man from Houston through a friend of mine. "Tom, I'm going on," I told him. "There are other men out there, and you don't intend to marry me. So I'm going to Houston for a date this weekend."

"Cancel the trip to Houston and spend the weekend with me, visiting my mother," he pleaded. That was all it took. We took the children with us to meet his mother in her new apartment in Fort Worth. Suddenly, my hopes of marriage to Tom looked bright.

After we returned from being paraded before Faye White, I knew we were irrevocably "lowercrust," and could never meet her "uppercrust" requirements.

Visiting his mother, I realized how much he struggled with pleasing her—just as Jim Bob struggled with pleasing *his* mother. I could see the rejection Tom felt. I knew he was confused about marrying me, knowing it would displease his mother. I wasn't sure Tom would choose to go against her wishes. I had to go on with my life.

The following Monday I went to see the counselor I had been consulting for some time. Tom went with me. As we began the session, I stated my feelings. "I've reached the point where I'm ready to go on with my life. Tom doesn't want to get married. I see no reason to stay in this relationship if we aren't going to get married. I want out," I explained.

Steve, the counselor, looked at Tom. "How do you feel about that, Tom?"

"I don't want to get married, but I'm not ready to call it off, either."

"Tom, you know Carol is a strong woman. This relationship won't wait. What are you going to do?" Steve asked.

"I don't like to be pushed into anything," Tom admitted.

"Tom," I responded, "I'm not pushing you. I'm just finished. I'm going on. I love you, and I want to build a life with you. But you don't want that."

"I'm not ready to remarry," he said, more to himself than to us.

Steve said softly, "I don't think Carol is questioning that. She's ready to leave you behind if that's how you feel. She understands. Tom, I don't know you, but I've been seeing Carol for some time. This woman isn't going to wait for you. If you want her, you're going to have to make a move—*now.*"

"I see."

After the session, we left in silence. Tom wasn't talking, and I felt I couldn't say any more. Sitting in the car at the red light, I was both relieved I had made a decision and sorry our relationship was over.

"Carol Nan, will you marry me this afternoon?" I heard Tom say, out of the blue.

Without hesitation, I answered, "Yes, Tom. I will."

"I'll call a Justice of the Peace when I get back to the office. Let's do it as soon as possible." And he kissed me.

I was on Cloud Nine! I skipped back into the office, but did precious little work. A bouquet of flowers came for me; it really was true! The telephone rang in about an hour, and my husband-to-be asked, "Can you meet me at the court house at four?"

"Yes, and thank you for the roses. I love you very much."

"I love you, too."

An Agreement Is Sacred

Tom White and I were married on November 9, 1970, exactly one year after my divorce from Jim Bob. I loved Tom and wanted to prove myself to him in every way; he would see he'd made a wise choice in marrying me, I assured myself.

Tom and I had a premarital agreement, and all the negotiations were settled long before the wedding. In the bedroom, over a period of months before the marriage, we defined the parameters. I often visualized Tom pulling out his little black book and recording another negotiated point.

Agreements are sacred to Tom White. If you renege on an agreement, you're weak, and Tom doesn't like weak people—certainly not a weak woman. "I felt trapped into the marriage with Susan because of her pregnancy," he often said. "I just don't want to be trapped again. You have two children, I have one; we don't need any more children."

"I'm not going to get pregnant, Tom," I assured him.

"If you do, will you get an abortion? I don't want another child."

"Sure, Tom. I'm not going to get pregnant. But if I do, I'll get an abortion," I agreed.

I saw the pain inside Tom and believed his suffering was caused by having been married to a weak woman. Thus, I allowed Tom to be demanding, because I was strong enough to meet his demands. I could also see how much rejection he felt from his mother. It would be an honor to be a strong woman standing beside this strong man. I would not let him down.

I wanted Tom White so badly that I didn't care what the premarital agreement said. The final terms of our negotiations were clear.

First, I would pay all the household bills; he would give me one hundred dollars per month, and pay the phone bill.

Second, if I became pregnant I would have an abortion. My two children, along with Tom's son, Trey, were enough. This part of the agreement I considered rather lightly simply because I never thought it would happen. With my experiences, I can't imagine why I thought that, but my oversight would come back to haunt me.

Third, my two children were my responsibility. He didn't want to be called "Daddy" by them—he was "Tom." I was to take care of them by myself.

Fourth, if we ever divorced, I had to pay all the legal expenses and ask nothing from him. He had been cleaned out once by Susan and wanted to be sure that never happened to him again.

Proving myself to Tom was very important. Whatever it took for me to be the perfect wife for him, I would do.

My life consisted of work at the hospital, cooking, cleaning the house, and taking care of three children each day. Trey stayed with us a lot during the week because one of Tom's former neighbors told him Trey was being left alone at night.

Professional opportunities were limited for Tom in Austin, so he began to search for a job elsewhere. We had been married about two years when the Frito-Lay corporation hired him.

We moved to Dallas in June, 1972, and lived in an apartment for three months until we bought a house. Tom settled into his job, and I went to work for Dr. Howard Wisner, as his office manager and operating room technician. Dr. Wisner used Garland Memorial as his primary hospital.

The Unexpected Happens

Between the dates of December 10 and December 12, 1972—and despite "precautions" intended to prevent it—I got pregnant.

Our premarital agreement notwithstanding, my deepest desire was to have Tom's baby. It was my third pregnancy, but the first one I was old enough—and in love enough—to truly enjoy. And yet, I feared Tom would reject me if I didn't honor item two of our contract.

I experienced some bleeding during the first weeks of my pregnancy, but the intensity of the mental and emotional struggle within me was worse—almost unbearable. I agonized over how to manage the issue with Tom.

My thoughts about the child were very warm. They were like a joyous, peaceful song playing inside me—in the midst of a gathering storm.

You are two weeks old, and I know you are there. I can feel you growing. All the hormones are changing in my body to let you grow and live. The changes are making me sick, but I don't care. You are going to be so special.

My other children are blonde and look like me, but you'll probably have a dark complexion, like your father. You'll have dark hair and dark eyes, too. I love you already!

I can feel you inside me, protected by my body, growing silently. I know you will be loved. Your sister is eight and your brother is ten, and you will be the baby, the last of my children. You and I are lucky; I'm twenty-eight years old, finally old enough to be the mother to you I have never been able to be to your brother and sister.

You are my secret. There will be problems when your father finds out, so you just grow quietly, and I'll take care of the rest. I'll protect you—somehow.

I'm making room for you in my body, even starting to glow on the outside. They say women are supposed to be prettier when they are pregnant. Some people even tell me I look pregnant, but it's too early—no one can really know but me.

I love your father so much, and because of our love you'll be cradled in love. You'll have a home with a mother and father who adore you, the way I was adored when I was born. You have a sister and a brother who will be excited to hear about your coming. Yes—there will be others who will wonder why I'm pregnant again, but I know you're a gift arising out of the love I have for your father.

Your coming will make us a family—the family I have longed for us to be all along. You don't understand this, but your sister and brother are mine from another marriage and your father is their step-father—but you will make us a family. Our lives will change because of you, but for the better. You will be the rallying-point of so many good things.

I hold my hand over my abdomen, where you are growing, to let you know I love you, and I want you very much. I can't wait to hold you in my arms. I'll breast-feed you, just so I can spend extra time with you, and I'll tell you all about this big new world you're entering.

You have fingers, toes, and a beating heart. You're alive. You have brain waves, and everything is growing according to plan. You're perfect. I just know it!

I also had what were for me some very strange thoughts about work and my career. Suddenly, the "good job" and the work-a-day world seemed so humdrum compared to being a full-time mother to this baby. I couldn't wait to begin devoting all my time to being a mother, a housewife, to putting my energy into my new baby, my daughter, and my son. Was I becoming weak—or discovering true strength?

The time had come to test the waters. Hoping for a miracle, I worked up the courage to tell Tom.

"Tom, I think I'm pregnant."

"What about the IUD?" he asked, immediately.

"It's still there, but I think I'm pregnant anyway."

"Are you going to the doctor?"

"Yes. You know I've been bleeding for over five weeks."

"Well, what about all those X-rays you've been exposed to in surgery?"

"I don't know; that's not good. There could be something wrong with the baby." I said it, but I didn't believe it—not really.

The conversation was over—for now.

It was a very trying time, wondering if he would push me to abort the child or decide to abort the marriage. The agreement I had entered into so lightly now weighed heavily on my heart.

Perhaps it sounds strange, but I was hoping for a miracle; yes, a miracle from God. After all, birth is a miracle, and life is formed out of the act of love.

I needed some support, some encouragement to help me deal with Tom, to circumvent the terms of our agreement. During my formative years in San Saba—Apple Pie, USA—babies were babies at conception, and abortions were out of the question.

During Christmas I told Aunt Nan I was pregnant, thinking she would surely help me. But she was sick at the time and wasn't able to muster any support for me. I told my mother and her mother, Grandmother Taylor, hoping they would encourage me, but they seemed indifferent. And my husband still wasn't saying a word. He had always said children were a liability—referring, I thought, to *my* children. Why did I think he would consider another one—even if it was *ours*—to be an asset?

What if he walked out on me? Running through my mind constantly was the thought, *How will I feel, with three children, living without Tom? How can I make it alone?* And I wondered how soon he would leave me if I didn't abort the child.

The bleeding continued into the sixth week. I finally went to see Dr. Harvey Johnson, a college roommate of Dr. Wisner's, for a checkup to confirm my pregnancy. I had met Dr. Johnson while working at the hospital for Dr. Wisner, and chose him to be my personal doctor because of his good reputation. Dr. Johnson examined me and told me my IUD was perfectly in place, that I wasn't pregnant, and that what I needed was a "D and C"—dilation and curretteage—to remove the IUD and stop the bleeding.

I can't tell you how relieved I was that I didn't have to make a decision about an abortion. The expert had spoken. And besides, if I were pregnant and he did a D and C, at least I would not bear responsibility for killing my child.

Surgery was scheduled for 7:00 A.M. the next day. I left Dr. Johnson's office, returned to work for a few hours, then checked into the hospital. The lab work was done that evening, in preparation for my procedure the following morning.

Early the next morning, the nurse informed me that Dr. Johnson needed to examine me again. *What in the world is going on?* I thought.

I was wheeled into an examining room with Dr. Johnson.

"Carol, you are pregnant, after all," he announced, soon after his examination.

"I told you I was," I replied.

"I can't do a D and C."

Now I was on an emotional roller coaster. My thoughts focused on my baby again. *We've been given a reprieve. See, no one listens to me. I knew you were there. But now they know, too. You're not safe anymore.*

A Choice Is Made

I had a choice to make—my child or my husband. After being discharged from the hospital, I called Tom at work.

"I'm not having surgery today."

"Why?"

"The pregnancy test is positive. I'm definitely pregnant."

There was silence. Not a word, only silence.

I told my friends at work I was pregnant, and they kept asking me, "What are you going to do?"

"Have an abortion." How did those words so easily come out of my mouth?

I started building a case to justify my future action. *I've been bleeding for six weeks now,* I reasoned. *That must mean there's a problem with the pregnancy. And what about the X-rays I've been exposed to? Wouldn't the baby be deformed?* But despite my attempts at self-justification, I hated myself, and there wasn't anyone to rescue me.

I can't do it, I decided. *The abortion has to be stopped. Dr. Johnson is my way out. He'll save me from myself. I'll go ahead and ask him for his opinion of abortion, and he'll just say, "No, abortion is wrong." After all, Dr. Johnson has a good reputation...*

Also, that should keep me safe with Tom. I'll just tell him I can't have an abortion—Dr. Johnson said so. Tom will see that I'm not weak, not reneging on my agreement.

For the second time in the first six weeks of my pregnancy, my personal rules allowed me to turn to some recognized authority for protection. First, I turned to God, praying for a miracle; second, to my highly professional doctor. A doctor who truly believes the Hippocratic

Oath would say, "How could you think of such a thing as abortion?" After all, doctors are supposed to work to prolong life, to protect and support life—not take it. Aren't they?

The Hippocratic Oath has been the ethical cornerstone of the medical profession since late in the fifth century, A.D. It states, "To please no one will I prescribe a deadly drug, nor give advice which may cause his death. Nor will I give a woman a pessary to procure abortion." A more modern version states, "I will maintain the utmost respect for human life from the time of conception; even under threat, I will not use my medical knowledge contrary to the laws of humanity. I make these promises solemnly, freely, and upon my honor."

"Dr. Johnson," I asked when I called, "what do you think about abortion? Tom wants me to have one. I hear they're doing them in New Mexico."

I was stunned beyond words when I heard Dr. Johnson's response. "You don't have to go anywhere; I do them all the time." He was a "secret" abortionist, and I didn't know it. Even through the telephone line he must have sensed my shock. "It's not a baby yet," he assured me, "it's only a glob of tissue."

That wasn't what I needed to hear. "Oh, well...we surely can't talk about this over the telephone," I managed, "because it's illegal. Do I come to your office, or—where do we meet to talk about this?"

"Oh, no problem," Dr. Johnson said. "Just bring in the father's urine; we'll give it to the lab for the pregnancy test, and it'll be negative, of course. I'll call the procedure a D and C, and your insurance will pay for it."

I learned that day that there are doctors...and there are abortionists.

On January 22, 1973, the Supreme Court ruled in favor of abortion in the *Roe vs. Wade* case, allowing a woman the right to privacy, the right to choose an abortion. Several states were already permitting abortions, but I didn't know it at the time.

But, did the "secret" abortionist know it? Was Dr. Harvey Johnson afraid of being found out by his existing clients, those who didn't need his "hush-hush" service?

Harvey Johnson made abortion sound so simple, so easy. After all, the baby growing inside me, conceived by me and the man I loved as the product of such precious intimacy, was just a glob of tissue.

I struggled with Dr. Johnson's "expert" opinion about abortion. My thoughts ran wild. I talked to the "glob of tissue"—really, to myself—as never before.

I really wanted to be your mother. I wanted you to have a father who loves you, a brother and sister who will love you instantly, love you so much that they'll carry you around and show you off to everyone.

Your dad won't talk to me about this. He doesn't want you. He thinks you'll only mess up the picture. We'd have diaper bags and 2:00 A.M. feedings, and things like that. I know you're not just a glob of tissue; you're growing inside me—a person. I know, too, that your growth has to stop—or I'll lose my husband, your father.

I have to pull myself together and be happy about this abortion. I'll just tell the children something went wrong with the pregnancy, so they won't find out the truth.

My last hope was gone; I saw no way out.

I didn't have enough trust in my relationship with Tom to challenge the agreement. I wanted the child, but I loved my husband. It was a choice between the baby I wanted and the husband I worshiped. If I told Tom I wanted the child, I would be showing weakness and breaking our premarital agreement—and agreements are sacred to Tom White.

The hour of decision had come. The time was close for the ultimate sacrifice—a blood sacrifice—which would prove my love for Tom. He would be sure of my love for him...but would I be assured of his love for me?

No matter how much I love you, I told the child, *your father doesn't want you. If I keep you, he won't want me. You are so little; it really won't hurt you. I'm so sorry—so very, very sorry.*

I made my final decision, consoling myself with this fact: Agreements are made to be broken, but love doesn't break them. I loved Tom. He wins—this time. And the child loses. That's just the way it had to be.

I made the most difficult phone call of a lifetime. "Dr. Johnson, let's do it—as soon as possible. When can I go in? Tomorrow? Yes, I'll be there."

When I checked into the hospital Thursday evening, February 15, 1973, Tom went with me and did his part; he provided the urine Dr. Johnson requested for insurance purposes, guaranteeing a negative pregnancy test. By that act, if by no other, Tom cast his vote for the abortion. Whether or not he wanted to accept involvement, that act guaranteed to me that he would face his judgment as surely as I would face mine.

Later that evening, I was alone; just me and the baby. I never felt so heavy or numb in all my life. *We are alone, now. I don't know what to say. What kind of mother am I to voluntarily take your life from you? I wish your dad would call me and say, "Stop!"—releasing me from the stupid promise I made.*

I want you, but if I violate my promise, your father will leave me. I still love him so much, and I really don't know you; please try to understand. Although there is plenty of room for you in my heart, there just isn't enough room for you in our home.

As I lay there, mentally preparing myself for the abortion, I irrationally wished for Tom to be transformed into a knight in shining armor who would race through the door of the hospital room and rescue us—the baby and me. I wanted to call Tom and beg, "Please don't make me do this."

But the words remained unspoken. What a tragedy for the unborn child—and for Tom, Joe Bob, Kelly...and me.

As they wheeled me into the operating room, I asked Jodie, the surgical supervisor, "How is the procedure listed on the schedule?"

"It's posted as an 'incomplete abortion,' which is the term for a spontaneous miscarriage that has not completely discharged all the pregnancy."

The operating room doctors and nurses were my co-workers at the hospital. Jan Batson, Dr. Johnson's scrub nurse, patted me and said reassuringly, "We're going to get this taken care of and get you back to work."

My third child was aborted at 7:00 A.M. Friday morning, February 16, 1973.

Friday had always been a special day for Tom and me, during our dating period and throughout our marriage. It was a time I always looked forward to with joy and fondness. But there was no joy that Friday; only heaviness and shame. Fridays would never be the same again.

When I woke up, my womb was empty. I felt the void where my child had been safely tucked away only a few hours earlier. Depression overwhelmed me; guilt engulfed me; tears flooded from my eyes. I felt too ashamed to call my mother, Grandmother Taylor, or Aunt Nan for comfort. I didn't think I deserved comfort for what I had just done.

My heart was broken. The joyful song of the life forming and growing within me was gone, along with the excitement and anticipation. I had nothing to sing about anymore.

But Tom's strong woman honored her sacred agreement. Carol, the strong one, did not show weakness, didn't welsh on the deal. The price was paid in full with the sacrifice of the life of our innocent, helpless child.

Death is so final. Death was the ultimate winner; not Tom, and not Carol.

Death.

6

....

A VICTIM OF THE BIG LIE

LIKE MANY OTHERS, I bought the big lie: "It's only a glob of tissue—not a baby."

And I was a victim of all the other lies: "Abortion is all right. After all, I do them all the time. It'll be so much simpler this way. We'll do it at the hospital and your insurance will pay for it. There's really nothing to the procedure; it'll only take a little while and then everything will be back to normal. You can have the abortion on Friday morning and go back to work on Monday." So easy. So convenient. No consequences.

On Friday morning, February 16, 1973, I voluntarily joined the society of post-abortive women. We were a very secretive society then, with one thing in common—the killing of our unborn children.

In 1973 not much was known about abortion and its effect on the other victims—the aborted child's mother, father, living siblings, grandparents, and other family members. Because of the secrecy surrounding abortion, there was no way of knowing the impact abortions were having.

But I can assure you my abortion served to further destroy my self-worth and compound my destructive habits toward my family, my co-workers, and ultimately toward all of society.

I take full responsibility for aborting my child, yet I also consider myself a victim of abortion. I was the victim of an abortionist, too—an entrepreneur in a budding industry that has experienced phenomenal growth since 1973.

Post-Abortion Syndrome

In the recovery room the truth really hit me: That "glob of tissue," that impersonal product of an accidental conception, was my aborted child. I had killed my baby, my child by Tom. I was supposed to nurture and protect that baby, but I killed it. Back in my hospital room, my mind and emotions were like a runaway train headed for a big crash.

What is it with me; why do I hurt so badly? I was told abortion was not supposed to be this painful or bother me this much. Why do I feel so depressed, now that I have liberated myself from motherhood? No two A.M. feedings, no dirty diapers. I thought the "freedom to choose" was supposed to make me feel better, even make me feel more like a woman. Why do I feel raped?

My mind and emotions continued to race. *The baby and I are the only ones who got hurt in this abortion. Tom escaped again. I must have a sterilization procedure done right now, so I will neither get pregnant nor ever hurt so badly again. Only then will I really be liberated.*

I imagined God would somehow punish me. *Oh no! God will take away Joe Bob or Kelly now, because I have killed my unborn child!*

I left the hospital feeling guilty, confused, and ashamed.

On the way home I picked up shrimp for our regular Friday "Funday" dinner. I had mixed emotions about facing my two living children. I wanted so badly to hold them and tell them how much I loved them and needed them, but what would they think if they knew what I'd just done? Could they tell by merely looking at me? I picked them up at the baby-sitter's house.

"Hi, urchins! How are you?" I hugged them, one in each arm, holding on too long for Joe Bob's comfort. He wiggled away, so I almost crushed Kelly hugging her.

"Fine, Mommy. How do you feel?"

"I feel fine. I'm glad to be home with you."

"How was your day, Kelly?"

"Okay."

"Joe Bob, how was your day?"

"Okay. Can I go out to play?"

"Sure. Kelly, what are you going to do?"

"I want to see if Jennifer is at home and wants to play."

"That'll be fine."

Normal conversation. The children didn't suspect that I had just committed murder. Life was normal for them, so I had to try to be normal, too. *Will they ever discover just what kind of mother I really am? They mustn't. They will never find out from me what I have done.*

The first thing I wanted to do was reach out to Tom, to ask him to help me fill the emptiness I felt inside—the emptiness created by the loss of the warm, tender affection I had been experiencing with the baby in my womb. Somehow, I had to replace that natural, instinctive love I had for our baby, that love which grew each day I carried our unborn child.

While preparing Tom's favorite shrimp dinner, I longed for him to make the first move, to hold me—thinking that now he would really love and comfort me, would empathize with me and appreciate what I had done for him. After dinner, my perfect performance required that I clean the kitchen quickly and efficiently, and get the children to bed. Then I went to our bedroom, hoping Tom would want to strengthen our bond of love, to fill the new emptiness within me. Would he reach out to me, even though we could not have sex?

"How do you feel?" he asked.

"I'm all right."

"How long will it be before we can make love again?"

His question infuriated me. *That's all he wants from me. He doesn't love me, doesn't respect me; and most of all, he doesn't understand what I have just done for him.* Aloud, I answered, "No sex for a week. Tom, I feel terrible and so depressed..."

"What's on TV tonight?" he asked.

Does he even hear me? I suppose I should be happy he doesn't go outside to one of his beloved automotive projects. At least he's staying inside with me. I feel so alone—in this king-size bed with this man I love, but who doesn't really seem to care about me.

"Tom, I'm really upset about this."

"About what? What do you mean?"

"The abortion."

"Carol Nan, we made the best choice we could, and we need to go on with our lives."

That was it. There was no reassurance or comfort to be had from him.

I felt very remorseful and had thought—maybe hoped—Tom was feeling the same way. But he wasn't. I couldn't believe the callousness of his words: *We made the best choice we could, and we need to go on with our lives.*

I quietly cried myself to sleep while the father of my aborted baby watched television. I was looking for his affirmation, but there was no acknowledgment that I had done anything special. It was all in a day's work. *We made the best choice we could...*

Despite my disappointment that night, I kept hoping Tom would change—would become a real husband to me and a father to my children.

It didn't work that way.

"Are you going to work on your car again tonight?" I'd ask him.

"Yes. I'm going to cover the dash of the Mercedes with leather. That should be about the last thing I do to it."

"So…what's the next project?"

"The Jaguar."

"Is there ever going to be any time for me?" I demanded, a shrill echo of my mother's voice. "I think you must have orgasms working on your cars. The cars come before everything else."

Out the door he would silently go—to his projects.

I needed a family unit more than ever before. Absurdly, I wanted to get pregnant again. I wanted a child with Tom, the only man I had ever spontaneously loved. But Tom had other things on his mind—things other than our family.

Finally, I gave up. The emptiness, the hurt, and the depression helped me decide to have the sterilization procedure done. I finally accepted the fact that Tom didn't want to have children; there would be no living children from our union.

As soon after my abortion as Dr. Johnson would consent to do the surgery, I surrendered the life-giving part of my femininity to my strong, destructive self. Pain begat more pain. I would never have another child.

My Path of Destruction

The thrill and excitement of being with Tom White had evaporated. The spark that once ignited my fire for him was gone. The joyful song inside me, created by our love, was silenced—and in its place came the comfortless knowledge, gained too late, of what Tom and I really had together: a cheerless, sterile business relationship. That was all.

Someone once said "Love is blind." Well, my blinders were finally off, and Tom's appearance had changed. He looked like a man who deserved to be humbled, to be punished . . . and I was just the woman for the job.

Two weeks after the sterilization process, I started the assault, using my old ally—sex. I began planning an affair. I had to prove to myself that I was lovable, to find someone to fill my emptiness inside. And I had to punish Tom.

What a mess I was! Unloved, unlovable, but desperately trying to prove otherwise; feeling guilty, yet unwilling to forgive. Acting so self-righteous as I went to work to mete out punishment on my partner in the sin we committed together against our innocent, helpless child.

I began an affair with a co-worker. Then I began another (one affair wasn't enough for me). I had many affairs, each one designed to wound Tom more deeply. He appeared to be taking his punishment like a man. He assured me he was not running around. After all—agreements are sacred to Tom. He even started taking more interest in caring for the children. Maybe my plan was working!

But my destructive pattern was not limited to Tom. I was subconsciously punishing myself, too. I began to change as many patterns in my life as I could.

Drinking had always been a man's thing to me; I had only taken a few drinks in my entire life. But now I had some new, liberated female friends who went drinking after work. So, at least once a month, I joined them...and got really drunk.

The first time I accompanied my friends, I didn't call Tom until after eight-thirty in the evening. "Tom, I had to work late with John, and I forgot to call you. I'm sorry. Can you go get the children?" Surely he could hear the music in the background.

"I picked up the children when I realized you were going to be late," he replied.

What a shock! Tom picked up the children by himself! I was delighted I hadn't called him. Now he knew how I felt when *he* didn't come home. "Have you and the kids eaten?" I asked.

"Yes. We've eaten."

"I'll be home soon," I lied. I wanted to finish the evening with my friends, and I did. I don't know what time I finally got home, but it was early the next morning. I was hung over the next day, but I showed Tom what it was like when he went out drinking. *At least I called at 8:30 to tell him. He never calls me,* I rationalized.

Work became my real "mister" and spending money became my new "mistress." I found solace in buying a new outfit when I got really depressed. That happened more and more often. I loaded up all my credit cards and soon got into a financial pinch.

I took a second job as a waitress at the Knights of Columbus hall. In the past, I had disdained waiting on tables. Now, the job became part of my self-flagellation. There was a side benefit, however; men noticed me, complimented me, and asked me out. My life with Tom was so negative, and the attention of all those men opened new doors in my mind. *Perhaps there is life for me after Tom White,* I thought.

Separation would be my final act to hurt Tom; nothing else I had done had succeeded in breaking him. I felt strong enough now to separate from him for a while, maybe six months. By then he was sure to come around.

"Tom, I think we should separate for a while," I suggested one evening.

"That would probably be good. I'll move out."

This is too easy, I thought. *But if Tom takes his punishment like a man, he can move back in for the summer while the children are with my parents. We can have the honeymoon we never had.* I had it all worked out.

Even Tom's mother called me. "Carol Nan, if he moves out, you'll never get back together with him. Isn't there some way you can work this out and continue to live together?"

If you only knew what your son has done to me, my thoughts screamed. *I killed our baby—my baby—for him, and he didn't even notice. I hate him for that. If he doesn't change, I don't want him to move back in.*

My last step before separation was to buy a new car. I picked out a color I hated—yellow—and financed it at a San Saba bank without Tom's help.

We separated in February 1974. If he accepted the final phase of my punishment and humbled himself, we would get back together; if not, I'd divorce him.

I Hit Bottom

It became a source of pride to me that I could sleep with a man and not care for him even slightly. If he tried to get close on his terms, I manufactured a cause for anger at him, to keep him from hurting me.

I wanted to compete with men, to compete for control of the relationship. I saw them on my terms, on my turf.

My spending habits worsened. When my credit cards reached the limit, I started borrowing money from friends, until their cards reached their limit also.

All my destructive ways pushed Tom further away. In the early spring of 1974, when it finally became clear that we weren't going to get back together, I sank into a deep depression.

Suicide would be my way out, I decided. A car wreck would be the way to do it; no one would ever know I was weak. Of course, I had to be certain the wreck was fatal—that was the tricky part.

Some other details had to be worked out as well. Who would take care of the children? I called my sister.

"Tooter, if something happens to me, will you take care of my children?"

"Sure. But how would I support them?"

"I have a life insurance policy; they'll get my social security, and Jim Bob will continue his child support."

I had it all figured out…except for one thing. If my sister kept the children, they would be reared in San Saba. I had no intention of letting Jim Bob Everett have the children. And Tom still saw the children as a liability. Three strikes and you're out. Suicide was not an option for me after all…unless I could get Tom to rescue me.

"Tom, I'm going to kill myself," I told him. "There's no reason to go on."

"You won't kill yourself," he said.

But he did call Dr. Blair, my psychiatrist, to see if he thought I was really suicidal. Finally, I went to see Dr. Blair.

"Your husband called to ask if I thought you would really kill yourself."

"What did you tell him?"

"I don't think you will."

"How can you be so sure I won't? I just might." I bridled at anyone telling me what I was or wasn't going to do.

In our sessions, Dr. Blair kept asking how I felt about him. I told him he was the doctor for my mind and nothing more. I thought he acted jealous when I told him I was dating a psychologist. He began to prescribe "mood elevators" so strong that when I took one at bedtime, I slept through the night and floated through the entire next day.

I saw Dr. Blair for about four months, then daily for the last month. It finally became so expensive I couldn't afford to see him anymore. By that time, I was hooked on Tofranil, and took it for two more years—with Dr. Harvey Johnson providing the prescription.

After a year of focusing my attention on Tom, I gave up my warped plan to "restore" him.

At the very bottom of the deepest pit of depression imaginable, I turned to Joe Bob and Kelly to help fill the emptiness in my life. I felt like such a failure as a mother; subconsciously, I was too ashamed to feel I deserved their love. Everyone else in my life had loved me only as long as they felt I deserved it. Why should my children not feel the same way?

Joe Bob and Kelly had witnessed their mother falling madly in love with Tom and had lived with the excitement between us for four years. They also witnessed the anger and hatred that grew between us after the abortion, not knowing why those feelings were there. They watched their mother run wild with other men without any explanation. Why should I expect them to be receptive to me now, when I had neglected them so long?

At the ages of thirteen and eleven, they were living with a drugged-up, mood-swinging, workaholic mother who was trying desperately to cope with depression. They watched their mother—once a good cook and housekeeper who took great pride in keeping their clothes nice—come to completely neglect domestic responsibilities. *Those are a woman's job*, I thought. And I just couldn't do them anymore.

I'd come home in a drugged fog and remark, "How nice that you cooked dinner, Kelly. It smells so good. Who cleaned the house?"

"I did," Joe Bob piped in.

"It really looks nice. Thank you."

I can just imagine how Kelly and Joe Bob felt trying to cook and clean the house, as I had once done for my mother. Trying to help their mother, thinking, hoping, and praying it would somehow help things between Tom and me. Oh, dear God! What webs we weave!

It was so painful, so guilt-inducing to spend time with the children, that I limited my involvement with them. I feared getting too close to them. If I did, they might discover my secret.

That June, as soon as school was out, I took the children to San Saba to stay with their grandparents for the summer. This gave me an opportunity to get my act together, to get out of the depression I was in and away from the psychiatrist.

Finding the Answer in Work

A saying of my father's helped me: "Get out there, sister, and go to work. Work hard; don't sit around and gripe, pout, or cry. Sister, you know where the money is. You know, sometimes I work twenty-four hours a day if I have to. You can do it, too. You have responsibilities. You have two children to raise by yourself. Your mother and I always put you kids first. Take good care of your family."

Work was my answer—hard work and a lot of it. What I needed was a challenging new job, a new career. My children needed a change, also.

"Mother, will you change your name back to Everett when you divorce, so it'll be the same as ours?" they begged.

"Yes, I will, kids." I started using my old name even before the divorce was final.

I still respected Tom's business mind, so I sought his advice about a career change. He was honest with me. "You'll never be happy until you're back in sales. That's where your real talent lies. Find yourself a job selling medical supplies. You understand the needs of doctors."

The next job had to be one where I could compete with men, bury them alive, and make a great living for myself and the kids.

I approached Chuck Osborn, owner of Physician's Supply Service, who sold medical supplies to the doctor's clinic where I worked. "Chuck, I have some sales experience and I want to get back into sales. I'd like to talk to you about a job."

He shook his head. "Carol, you know I can't talk to you as long as you're working for Dr. Wisner. That would be a conflict of interest." Then he winked and said, "But, let me know when you leave. I think I can put you to work."

After I gave my notice, I called Chuck. "Now I'm unemployed— and I want to talk to you about a job."

"Come on over. You need to meet my partner, John. Can you be here at ten o'clock today?"

"Yes. I'll be there."

In the interview, Chuck remarked, "Carol, you know there are no other women selling medical supplies in this area. You should be able to get a lot of business just because you're a woman."

I wasn't planning to make my living based on my femininity—but if it would help, why not?

"I'm sure you'll be a good salesperson aside from being a woman, but that asset won't hurt you," he continued.

If they only knew how I felt about my womanhood.

"We only have one other employee—our sales manager, John Scott. We can give you a draw of four hundred and fifty dollars per month, plus forty percent of your gross profit from sales—much higher than any other comparable company in the area. Most companies pay only thirty to thirty-three percent of gross. You can make a lot of money, Carol, if you're willing to work."

Work was my middle name. *Get your checkbook ready, Chuck.*

I continued to scrub part-time for Dr. Wisner for several more months, and to work for the Knights of Columbus as a waitress.

As I began my new career, I had to close the final chapter of my old life. My divorce with Tom had to be finalized in order to shut the door on the past four-and-a-half years. I had to honor the fourth part of our premarital agreement. I would pay all of the legal expenses for the divorce and ask for nothing from him in the way of a settlement.

My marriage to Tom finally ended in August, 1974. I called him and tearfully told him the divorce was final. "Tom, you're a free man. Our divorce was final at about half past nine this morning. I paid for everything. I held up my end of the agreement."

Tom's voice was strange. I didn't know if it was relief or sorrow. All he said was, "Thank you for calling. I love you."

"I love you, too."

How had this happened? Tom was legally free, but always in my heart the door remained open for him to enter my life again.

It had been an emotional meat grinder for both of us. As for me, I had never experienced such highs in a relationship—nor such lows. And while I vented my anger outwardly, Tom suppressed his.

The loss of two loves—my unborn child and my "heart-stopper" husband—along with the loss of my female life-giving ability, created an unbearable emptiness. I had been deeply hurt by reaching toward the wrong sources to be filled again—setting me up to be even more destructive.

What next? How many victims would my abortion claim?

7

THE ABORTION
BUSINESS BECKONS

I BEGAN A NEW CHAPTER in my life in the fall of 1974. I had no idea how my past would figure in my future. An unseen hand had written a script just for me, designed a leading role for someone with my exact credentials.

But this was no make-believe drama; this was real life. This leading lady would wreak havoc on her helpless audience. It would be as though I had never had an abortion, as though I had forgotten all the pain I suffered as a victim.

In my wildest imaginings I could never have fathomed the door that would be opened to me—one that would make me rich, would enable me to do all the things I ever dreamed of doing for my children and myself.

This starring role required a leading lady with my special qualities:
- An insatiable craving for attention; a woman who loved the limelight.
- An unscrupulous woman who didn't mind bending the rules.
- A strong woman with a tireless work ethic who needed to make a lot of money.
- A woman who understood doctors, who had experience in running a medical clinic.
- A woman who knew a closet abortionist longing to go public—lured by the big bucks.
- A feminist; a silent member of the post-abortive women's society.
- A woman who knew how to market and how to sell; one who could relate to women, manipulating their feelings, if necessary.
- A woman with a strong dislike for men and a desire to use them, even to punish them, control them.

It seemed too good to be true, "a match made in heaven." My dysfunctional heritage and life experiences would merge with a phenomenally lucrative opportunity. I would no longer have to dream about being rich—I *would* be rich.

I was thirty years old, single, and living in the midst of a sexual revolution spearheaded by the women's liberation movement. Women were talking openly to each other about the injustice of a male-dominated society that saw women as being inferior to men. They were decrying their emotional weakness, a characteristic of our sex, which kept them from winning.

I was ahead of the game. I had a lot to teach women; I was on the cutting edge of something big. I was also very lonely, unable to relate effectively with men or women. I was having a real identity crisis, struggling to be somebody, *anybody* but the person I had been.

In my new search for significance, I initially focused on becoming the top sales person in the medical supply field. I continued to help Dr. Wisner in his office and to work as a waitress for the Knights of Columbus. The drug Tofranil was my special friend as I tried to live with myself and keep up my punishing work schedule. The kids were getting everything they needed—except attention from their mother.

My income from medical supply sales grew from a base of four hundred and fifty to one thousand five hundred dollars per month over the next two years. And there was more money to be made at J.D.'s After Dark, a bar on Harry Hines Boulevard. I left the Knights of Columbus hall and went to work at J.D.'s in November 1975.

I continued to see Tom, my ex-husband, while using other men. The children continued to get more attention from their grandparents than from me. And I continued to try to prove my worth in dollars, like a man.

In the meantime, John, Chuck's partner in Physician's Supply Service, acquired a new account—one that paid top dollar for our equipment and supplies without questioning the price. John and Chuck investigated the business and soon discovered it was an abortion clinic.

A Lucrative Business Opportunity

The Women's Center, located in a high-profile Dallas area, was owned by Dr. Sam Greene. Greene got his start doing abortions on women referred to him by the East Texas Pastoral Council—long before *Roe vs. Wade.* In February 1973, he opened his clinic and began doing legal abortions.

Dr. Greene was not the only closet abortionist to go public after *Roe vs. Wade.* Most of the back-alley abortionists and profiteers opened clinics. Billboard and newspaper advertising began to scream *ABOR-TION!,* always with a prominent telephone number. Women gladly lined up to exercise this newfound freedom that was revolutionizing sex and womanhood.

Chuck and John established a good rapport with the operators of the clinic, gained an understanding of the abortion business, and found it to be lucrative. They decided the money was too good to pass up.

Late in 1975, they went into the abortion business themselves, using Chuck's Aunt Sue, an R.N., as the front person. They opened their first clinic in Fort Worth. Within a year they owned three abortion clinics—in Fort Worth, Lubbock, and Beaumont.

The first year Chuck and John operated their clinics, I was not involved in any way. I was concentrating my efforts on medical supply sales. One of the first doctors to open an account with me was my personal Ob-Gyn, abortionist, and drug purveyor, Dr. Harvey Johnson. His door was always open to me, and I looked forward to seeing him because he made me feel good.

I felt a strange attachment to Harvey. He seemed to have a way with women—at least he could sense what *I* wanted. He touched me a lot, sprinkled his conversation with terms of endearment, and made me feel special and desirable.

One Friday afternoon Chuck approached me. "Carol, I need a doctor to do abortions tomorrow morning in Fort Worth. Do you know anybody who might be willing to cover it for me?"

I immediately thought of Harvey Johnson and called him. "You know Chuck Osborne, don't you—owner of the medical supply company? Well, he owns several abortion clinics and needs a doctor to help him in Fort Worth tomorrow. Are you interested?"

"Yes," Harvey quickly agreed.

"Here he is, then. I'll let you talk to him." I put Chuck on the phone.

Dr. Harvey Johnson's career in free-standing abortion clinics had been launched—by yours truly.

Then, on June 12, 1976, I received a phone call from my mother.

"Tooter is gone," she said in a toneless voice. "She drowned. How soon can you get here?"

"I'll leave just as soon as I can get my car out of the shop."

We were later told she broke her neck by diving into the waters of the San Saba River, where we had been diving all our lives. This time it was fatal.

The loss of my sister deeply affected both of my parents, so much so that I began to feel we all would have been better off if I had been the one killed. She left behind her six-year-old son, Cal, for my parents to rear. It were as though Daddy finally had the son he had always wanted. But I felt more displaced than ever, and I felt my two children were being pushed aside.

Just before Tooter's death, I finally stopped using Tofranil. The news of her death, and the guilt I felt because of my deep-seated jealousy, gave me the excuse I needed to start using it again.

I struggled with her death for several months, angry at her for leaving with unfinished business between us. I never got to tell her I was sorry for being jealous of her, nor was I able to tell her how much I truly loved her. What a tragedy for two sisters to grow so far apart, then suddenly be separated by death, never to resolve their differences!

I was furious at God when Tooter died. I had been sending my tithe regularly for about two years at the time of her death, but I had quit the month before. I fancied that God was playing the same old game of "invisible" sin Daddy played—punishing me with the death of my sister because I stopped sending my tithe to the church.

After Tooter's death I spent a lot of time in San Saba taking care of her grave—planting grass and flowers. I lost touch with everything, including my work ethic. Then Chuck meddled with my commission structure. I quit the medical supply business and went to work with a heavier schedule at J.D.'s After Dark. I spiralled into debt and depression, using Tofranil heavily.

In September, Chuck called me. "Carol, I'd like for you to come back to work. I'm sure we can iron everything out."

I swallowed my pride and went back to him.

Later that year, Chuck gave me a new opportunity. "Carol, how would you like to make some extra money? For any abortion referral you get from doctors, I'll pay you twenty-five dollars."

He knew I needed the money. And so, I took my first step toward becoming the leading lady in the abortion industry.

The plot thickened between Harvey Johnson and me. Right after my sister's death, he made me an offer. He and some other doctors had started North Texas Doctor's Radio, a beeper and answering service.

"How would you like to sell beepers for me?" he asked. "You can sell our service to the doctors you call on. It'll help both of us," he insisted.

It was a natural fit with my other business, and a nice way to make some extra money. "Okay, Harvey," I agreed. I sold beepers for several years, supplementing my income. Harvey tried to get me involved in several other business ventures with him, but I declined.

Then he made the big pitch. "Carol, how would you like to go out to dinner with me?"

I was stunned but receptive. "Sure, Harvey. When?"

"How about Friday night?"

I was all set for a big evening when he called, late Friday afternoon. "Something came up at the hospital. We'll have to postpone our date to another time."

"That's okay, Harvey. Some other time." I decided he had opted to reserve me for "business-only" purposes, and that was fine with me.

Harvey fit many of my criteria for my next mate: a good provider, tall, sensuous. But with all those qualities came the heightened possibility of losing him. He had too many opportunities with other women. A romantic interlude was not worth the risk if I was going to have a working relationship with him.

The strange attachment I felt toward Harvey strongly resembled my attachment to Tom. It was as though I were still connected to both of them.

Maybe that's the way it is—people with hidden, shameful pasts who collaborate in wrongful acts have to stick together. Maybe we know we're accepted by one another, that we're just as good as our cohorts. We feel so unclean and disgraced around others because we know nothing of their dark sides. Maybe if we knew their secrets, we could all get together and stop feeling so badly about ourselves. Maybe then we could be free from our bondage to a limited, "guilty" few.

As time passed, I found myself wanting more and more to please

Harvey. I knew he would reward me; he owed me. Harvey could be my ticket to a good lifestyle—without the sexual price tag.

Harvey's business consultant, a man named Wayne Byles, ran North Texas Doctor's Radio. I first met Wayne in 1976 when I started selling beepers for them. I made sure I got along with him because I wanted to use Harvey to catapult my career.

In early 1977, things blew up at North Texas Doctor's Radio, and Wayne left the company. Chuck and John had split up their partnership by this time. Harvey had earlier introduced Wayne to Chuck, and that gave Wayne the opening to talk to Chuck about going to work with him.

Wayne joined Chuck as his business manager and set up a new holding company, called Docta, Inc., for all of his businesses. By now, everyone at Physician's Supply Service was paranoid about Wayne; he had the reputation of being a "hit man" for corporations, a reputation he spread himself. "Sometimes that's what it takes to get the job done," he'd explain.

When Chuck and John ended their partnership, Chuck retained ownership of the Fort Worth abortion clinic and Physician's Supply Service, so Chuck went to work immediately to open an abortion clinic in Dallas.

Patty, Chuck's wife, set up the new Dallas clinic, and Chuck used his secretary, Joan, to assist her. I can remember Joan saying things like, "I wonder how many fingers and toes we put down the disposal today?"

Patty began to change, right before my eyes. She had always been so nice and genuinely friendly to everyone, but she became hostile and even paranoid, thinking everyone was after them. Chuck began to have excruciating headaches, and Patty developed other health problems.

Referral Centers

Nevertheless, Chuck saw a real opportunity to capitalize on the sexual revolution. He determined to do two things. First, he would open non-profit centers under the pretense of offering sexual counseling for women, with the real purpose being free pregnancy testing that would lead to abortion appointments for the clinics. Second, he would develop key relationships with the leaders and strong advocates of the women's movement in the area, using their influence to get abortion referrals.

Late in 1978, I realized I had to make more money. My income from medical supply sales was not enough. Chuck and I had a heart-to-heart talk. "Chuck, I can't make an adequate living selling medical supplies. With two children about to enter college, I have to start thinking about the future," I told him.

"Just work harder. You can make more money."

"No. As much as I love working for you, I am submitting my resignation. I have to find another job."

"How much money do you need to make?" he asked.

"My monthly expenses are currently two thousand, fifty-seven dollars."

"Well, some other opportunities exist within our corporate structure, related to the abortion clinics. We have a non-profit corporation, sanctioned by the IRS, which will enable us to open a chain of facilities we're calling Advisory Referral Centers. The centers will offer free sexual counseling and pregnancy tests. It'll mean some travel, but only limited overnight stays. Could you leave the children overnight occasionally?"

"Yes, they're almost old enough to leave alone. And I'd love to travel some. Where would this business be located?" This sounded interesting.

"The main office will be here, with the first branch office to be located in Shreveport, Louisiana. Then we'll go into Tyler, Irving, or the Mid-Cities, Abilene, Waco—any other areas we see generating abortions for our clinics. This could be a great job for you, Carol. Give me some time to work it out, and don't make any rash decisions. Keep on working hard at selling medical supplies, and come back in two weeks. I think we can work something out."

With high anticipation, I went to the corporate offices two weeks later. Chuck seemed excited as he spelled out the details for me.

"Carol, Wayne and I have been talking, and I think I have a good offer for you. I want you to be the new director of our Advisory Referral Centers. Your job will be to open and operate Advisory Referral offices in key locations. ARC will advertise sexual counseling and pregnancy tests—both free. Remember, we're mainly interested in the pregnancy tests, because we can funnel the pregnant women into our clinics in either Dallas or Fort Worth. We'll pick up a lot of business that we would otherwise miss." He paused. "You'll be paid two thousand, fifty-seven dollars per month, plus expenses. You'll love it."

"How much travel will be involved?"

"You'll determine that. Basically, you need to be in each location weekly until the staff is hired, trained, and the referral base is established. You'll also need to make contact with all the 'do-gooders' in the area, to let them know we're there to provide free sexual counseling and pregnancy tests.

"The fact that our services are free will attract high school counselors and social workers alike. The fact that abortions are no longer paid for by the state or the federal governments will mean you can get referrals from welfare agencies, also. They'll be glad to send you their clients for pregnancy tests, and we can counsel the pregnant women on where to go for their abortion.

"We've developed some literature, a logo, and Bob Roth has written some public service announcements which you can get broadcast free on the radio. Because ARC is non-profit, no one will ask questions, and we get free advertising for our pregnancy tests.

"Take these brochures and read about ARC. You're a good salesperson. You'll have no trouble at all setting these up. We want to have seven centers open as soon as possible. They'll really build our abortion business.

"We've already started the clinic in Shreveport, Louisiana. We hired the wife of the attorney general to cut through the red tape. We're ready for business over there.

"When can you go to Shreveport to work with the two part-time employees? They've already been trained to do pregnancy tests and counseling. You just need to meet them."

The more he talked, the more interested I became. This could be just what I was looking for. "I have some things to wrap up with PSS," I told him. "I can go to Louisiana the week after next." I had just taken the second step toward my starring role.

I went to work as director of the Advisory Referral Centers in January, 1979. The concept worked well, providing many referrals to Chuck's abortion clinics.

The business plan called for me to open centers in cities without abortion clinics, usually in conservative areas that would not allow an abortion clinic to operate. It was easy for me to step right in and begin to use the resources of the feminist movement to build the network of Advisory Referral Centers; Chuck was already using several big names in the movement. It was a natural connection for our business.

Director of the North Dallas Women's Clinic

Chuck and I were comfortable together, but I never trusted Wayne. Nor did he trust me—mainly because I didn't fear him and would go directly to Chuck with problems. Chuck never advised me to work through Wayne, and I think that bothered him, too.

I set up the Shreveport, Tyler, and Irving ARC offices. The first week Irving was open for business, a call came in from Wayne.

"How are things going over there, Carol?"

"Fine. I'm just settling in. I think we have a great location—we're on Highway 183 near two high schools. We should see a lot of girls."

"Carol," he said, "I need to have you come to North Dallas Women's Clinic. The director is no longer with us, and I need you to run things until I can find a replacement. Can you come?"

"Yes. I'll be right over."

The third step.

Wayne had never been an ally. If he was going to work with Chuck, however, I wanted him to be at least neutral, if not my friend. I was excited to have the opportunity to gain Wayne's trust—without too much risk, since it was a temporary situation.

But temporary soon became permanent.

"Carol, how would you like to run the front of the clinic?" Wayne asked after a few weeks.

"I'd love it, Wayne."

The fourth step.

Wayne was overseeing the abortion business, and my old friend, Harvey Johnson, was the medical director. They wanted me to handle the marketing and run the front office. I did a quick survey of the situation and determined I was sitting on a potential gold mine.

Greed—the love of money and the things I could get with it—blinded me, just as it did Harvey, Chuck, John, and Wayne. I was one of them now, a committed abortionist who would use whatever means were available to get a woman to have an abortion...and pay well for the privilege.

I would like to say I took the job to help women, but I can't make even such a poor plea as that. I did it for money, nothing more.

Numbers were the name of the game from a sales perspective, and I quickly saw many ways the numbers could be improved.

"Chuck, if we make just a few changes, we can greatly increase our business."

"What would you suggest, Carol?"

"First, we need to utilize the facility every day, with abortions being done continually. Harvey has to find some more doctors to help cover the clinic all day, every day. I'll book in the patients. Second, we can make a few changes in our telephone techniques; I think that putting more emphasis on our professionalism will increase our numbers."

"Go ahead and implement your changes." Chuck was all for improving business.

He called every day. "How are things going, Carol?"

"We're still not busy enough during the first part of the week. We need a doctor here all day Mondays and Tuesdays. We could do a lot more procedures with two more abortion days."

I drove to the corporate office for a weekly meeting with Chuck and Wayne. Chuck and I would talk; Wayne asked questions.

In one of the weekly meetings, Chuck said, "Carol, we want to be the Neiman-Marcus of abortion clinics in this area. North Dallas Women's Clinic needs to be warm, nicely furnished, staffed with caring people. The big difference between North Dallas Women's Clinic and the other abortion clinics in town is that we're in the high-rent district—North Dallas. That alone demands a higher-quality environment. I want you to furnish the waiting room and recovery room. Make them look really nice. Buy lots of plants and things like that." I was happy to oblige.

The business more than doubled. Chuck leased additional space and set up an office for himself at the clinic—he liked to be part of the action.

At lunch together one day, Chuck openly said, "You know, my income has gone from ten thousand to one hundred and twenty-five thousand dollars the first year in the abortion business. There's so much money to be made! Carol, you've been quite an asset at the clinic, acting as my eyes and ears. You've helped increase our bottom line."

The number of abortions performed at the clinic was less than one hundred and fifty when I started. The first partial month I was in charge, we had 168, the biggest month NDWC had ever had. We were now doing well over three hundred abortions a month, soon to reach four hundred. The growth in the business was a direct result of my hard work, six days a week. I deserved more than just a salary—I wanted part of the business. At the right time, I'd ask for it. I went away from that lunch meeting with dollar signs in my eyes.

Figure it out: Chuck had offered to pay me twenty-five dollars for every abortion referral I funneled to him when I was selling medical supplies. Now, I was running the clinic for a salary of $2,057 per month; his income was more than six times that. He had made a good deal in bringing me in to run his Dallas operation.

Kelly was barely fourteen when I first brought her in to help me in the clinic. I wanted to teach her how to be aggressive, assertive, and hard working. I thought she needed to learn that women have to work harder than men to avoid being second-class citizens.

She wasn't allowed to be involved in extra-curricular activities at school; she had to learn how to get ahead in life. I taught her how to sell abortions and how to handle the girls when they came into the clinic. She was good, really good, right from the start.

But regardless of how well she did things, Joe Bob got the affirmations, not Kelly. He was doing well athletically, socially, financially, and scholastically. Kelly was just doing a girl's job, helping her mother. I even managed to get Joe Bob a contract to clean the clinic in January 1980.

The clinic in Fort Worth was having some problems, and I was asked to go solve them. I took old reliable Kelly with me to help when she could.

Another abortion clinic in Fort Worth burned and had no place to send its patients, so I made a deal with the director to pay them twenty-five dollars for each abortion they referred to us until they could get back in business. Soon, the Fort Worth clinic was doing over four hundred abortions a month. Chuck was delighted—he and Wayne were taking the credit for the success.

PR and Marketing Advances

Once, at our weekly meeting, Chuck announced, "Carol, I want you to move up to public relations. You'll be able to establish a broader base of referrals, and you can work for both the Dallas and Fort Worth clinics."

I put on my PR hat and got creative. Early on, I noticed that many girls claimed they were raped, but they had not reported anything to the police or gone to a hospital. I had an idea that I thought would help us build our business to a higher level.

In one of our weekly meetings, I said, "Many of the women come in alleging they were raped, but they have neither reported it to the police nor gone to the hospital. I think we can get a lot of publicity if we have a press conference announcing that we will do abortions free for rape victims if they report it to the authorities. The percentage of conceptions in actual rapes is very low, and with the conditions attached, I don't think we'll do many free abortions. But we'll get a ton of free publicity!"

"Who'll go on television to talk about it?" Chuck protested. "I won't, and Wayne won't. I hate television cameras!"

"I'll go on television," I said. "We'll have the press conference right in the clinic, with coffee and donuts. We'll give the news media a tour and get prime-time coverage," I pledged.

"Which doctor will do the free abortions?"

"I'll talk to Harvey; he'll do them."

"Okay. Sounds like a good idea. Do it, Carol!"

Just as I had promised, we got prime-time news coverage at 6:00 P.M. and 10:00 P.M. Also, several newspapers and radio stations picked it up. I personally called on all of the "do-gooder" organizations in town and let them know. We received lots of good, free publicity!

"Carol, that was great!" they said, ecstatic at the success of the free-abortion gambit. "We got thousands of dollars of free advertisement that we could never have paid for! Great idea!" Chuck was thrilled.

We never did a single free abortion for a rape victim.

Chuck could see great value in my marketing abilities. Wayne didn't think the Fort Worth clinic was marketing aggressively enough. So we designed a "central booking" plan now used by other abortion providers. The Fort Worth staff couldn't sell abortions, but the Dallas staff could, supervised by me. All of our yellow page ads showed a single "800" number. When the calls came into the Dallas clinic, the women were sold on our service and directed to the appropriate clinic—Dallas or Fort Worth.

Directing a clinic involves more than marketing and selling abortions. In back is the medical end, and the front is the booking and business end—the money end. I was responsible for the front.

It was always difficult to find and train telemarketers who could call themselves "counselors" while selling abortions. "We're helping women," I had to remind them constantly. Those who didn't buy my pitch quickly left.

I started to believe my own rhetoric. I had to be convincing in order to persuade my telephone counselors. But each time I met with Chuck, I was quickly snapped back to reality—we were in business to make money, a lot of it.

There were always complications in the back end, but I was no stranger to complications, having assisted Dr. Wisner in surgery.

Dr. Leggett, a first trimester abortionist, worked for us in the Dallas clinic on Thursday mornings. A beautiful, blonde twenty-year-old girl once came in for a procedure. She was deaf. Dr. Leggett did her abortion and sent her to recovery. She continued bleeding, and her uterus did not contract as it should. The doctor checked her again and discovered, in his words, "She was having twins, and I only got one of them."

Another abortion procedure had to be done, but the young woman was scared and didn't understand why she had to have another procedure. We never told a woman she was pregnant with twins, because she might change her mind. Because of our problem in communicating with her, however, Dr. Leggett told her the truth, "You had twins."

To be honest, I never believed Dr. Leggett. I thought he just missed the baby the first time.

I held her hand for the second procedure. I will never forget the fear in those big, blue eyes as she underwent the second abortion in one day—with only a very light tranquilizer, since we were out of anesthesia. She remained very still and never screamed.

I was on a date one evening when my beeper sounded. Chuck informed me there was a complication in Fort Worth. The doctor had perforated a fifteen-year-old girl's uterus and had pulled her colon through her vagina. She was in John Peter Smith Hospital having surgery when I got there.

The family was very calm when I arrived, blaming themselves. What an opening! I let the mother continue blaming herself for her daughter's problem and made sure the clinic assumed no responsibility whatever. The doctor emerged and explained that he had repaired the uterus, that she might be able to have children in the future.

I left feeling very confident the family would not file a lawsuit, but would carry the blame themselves.

This experience taught me a valuable lesson for the future: A successful abortion clinic needs doctors willing to put their license on the line in the coverup of botched abortions. That's the only way to keep families from filing lawsuits. There is something almost god-like about a doctor coming out of the mysterious surgical unit with his scrub suit on, giving his report to the family. They will rarely question his truthfulness—they just want to know if everything's going to be all right.

The abortionist and the abortion provider need good cover from their physicians. In my mind, this meant I needed to be good to Harvey, if I intended to advance to stardom in the business.

By the end of 1979, I was doing my job well and feeling smug about it. It was time, I concluded, to ask for an equity interest in the business. Wayne and Chuck really needed me, and Tom, my ex-husband, advised, "You've helped build the business. Look at the records you have on your calendar alone. I would definitely ask for an equity interest. You deserve it."

This wasn't as easy to do as I'd hoped.

I went to Chuck and said, "I've more than doubled your business since coming on board. I want an equity interest."

"No," he said, without an instant's hesitation. "My family owns all the stock in this corporation. That's not going to change."

But I knew I had helped build his business and that I could do the same thing for myself. Chuck didn't realize who he was dealing with. I knew two could play this game. I also knew Harvey would come with me, and I knew he and Wayne wanted to get back into a working relationship.

In May 1980, I placed my own half-page ad in the *Yellow Pages* for 1981. I would be in business for myself with a well-moneyed partner by October 1, 1980. It was just a matter of learning everything I could and biding my time until I was ready to leave.

In June, Chuck called me. "Carol, the *Dallas Times Herald* wants to do an interview. Will you do it? I know you can do it, Carol. Just make like a 'do-gooder.'"

"Okay, Chuck."

I was interviewed in my office at the clinic.

"Why are you at the clinic?" the interviewer began.

"We're helping women have safe, legal abortions," I said, spouting the standard line.

"Isn't this a business?" the reporter persisted.

I was feeling so confident that I relaxed my guard and answered honestly. "Of course it's a business." Chuck's phrase came to mind. "We want to be the Neiman-Marcus of abortion clinics." Immediately, I knew that was a bad answer.

After the interview, I called Chuck and told him what I'd said. "Chuck, I want to refuse to let them publish my remarks," I insisted.

"Carol, don't worry. Everything will be all right."

The reporter printed my comments, quoting the exact words I'd heard from Chuck. On the printed page, they appeared crass. My honesty earned us top coverage—and bottom PR marks.

The headline on the inside page read, "Director Says 'Yes, This Is a Business.'" Chuck was horrified. My prideful but truthful answer got me fired two weeks after the news report came out.

He gave me three months notice—July, August, and September. That was perfect: My pre-placed ad in the *Yellow Pages* was set to break in October. All I needed was the money backing and I would be ready to take center stage.

In my time with Chuck, I had added item Number Nine to the list of my special qualities: a woman with experience in marketing and selling abortions, and running an abortion clinic. With this added dimension, I was ready for success, for the big leagues!

The Scarlet Lady was about to debut.

8

DRIVEN BY AMBITION

GREAT PERFORMANCES require hard work, but they result in recognition and reward. Performers risk disappointment and endure pain to enjoy their moment in the limelight.

At the age of thirty-five, I still craved the kind of attention from my daddy that I lost as a preteen. If I worked hard now, just as Daddy advised me to, I was sure I would get recognition and reward. Maybe I could even recapture my father's attention and win back his affection.

I was about to make my big push to become the queen of the abortion industry. I knew this risked more disappointment and pain. However, I felt well-equipped to handle the task. Memories of being queen of the May Fete at age two and a princess at age sixteen were enough to make me willing to pay whatever price success required.

When Chuck gave me notice in July 1980, I had three months to find a financial backer before Harvey and I could open the business we had decided to call Abortion Advisory Clinic. The half-page ad with Southwestern Bell was scheduled to appear in October 1980. Harvey helped me select the name for the new clinic, so I knew he was committed to join me when the time was right.

Just as soon as I found someone who expressed interest in becoming the financial partner, I went straight to Harvey. "I have someone who may be willing to finance the opening of the clinic. Do you want to meet with us?" I asked.

"Let me talk to Wayne about it and get back with you, Carol," he replied.

I anxiously waited for Harvey to respond.

"Carol, Wayne and I would like to meet with you and Rhett." Rhett was the money man. "Can you set it up?"

"Sure, Harvey. I'll get back to you."

I set up the meeting in Wayne's office, and Wayne did the negotiating for us with Rhett. Negotiations broke down, and Rhett backed out. I was crushed that things hadn't worked out the way I had hoped.

October passed without any success in finding someone to finance me. My expectation of opening my own clinic crumbled.

When my job with Chuck ended, I swallowed my pride and returned to selling medical supplies for International Medical Sales, Inc. I was making adequate money, but my heart was no longer in medical supply sales. I yearned to be back in the abortion business, making scads of money—certainly, more money than I could ever make selling medical supplies.

On a Saturday morning in November, Harvey called and laughingly said, "I saw Joe Bob's picture on the front page of the *Dallas Morning News* sports section. Looks like he missed a tackle!" Good old Harvey, never one to let an opportunity for criticism go by.

"By the way," he continued, "I took over the Mockingbird clinic from Dr. Robinson in August. He couldn't run it long distance. I helped him out of a potential lawsuit by admitting a patient for him. He made me an offer which allowed me to buy the clinic by assuming his debt.

"Carol, several people you know are down there working with me on Saturday. I can't afford to pay you right now, but why don't you come on down and work for the fun of it? Get Kelly to come, too. It'll be like old times."

Working with Harvey Johnson for free was certainly not my idea of fun, but I agreed anyway.

When I hung up the phone, I was really hurting inside. I couldn't believe what I'd heard! Then I got angry. Harvey had excluded Wayne and me from his deal. If I'd had the opportunity, I would certainly have included him. How could he have the gall to ask me to work for him for free?

It was February 1981 before I worked up the courage to visit Harvey at his new clinic. Kelly and I worked one Saturday, as I promised. It was clear to me Harvey wanted to use us as he was using others. Once more, I felt betrayed by a man I had trusted.

Harvey was running the Dallas Medical Ladies Clinic himself and doing everything as cheaply as possible, using anyone he could get to help him, including his Garland office staff and nurses from his regular practice. He had no management staff and was doing no advertising. He was doing all the abortions himself, on Wednesdays and Saturdays.

I went home that Saturday, after working all day for free, asking myself, *Why didn't Harvey invite me into the deal? I'm shocked. Doesn't he realize how much I can help him? Harvey has abandoned me and left me out in the cold. The one abortionist I wanted most to work with doesn't need me after all.*

But great performers prove their grit by rising above disappointment. I was down, but not out. Harvey Johnson had not heard the last from me.

Back in Business

On one of our dates, Lonnie, my banker boyfriend, jokingly asked me, "Why don't you go to work for Dr. McPhearson and help him solve the problems in his abortion clinic? He's putting twenty-seven thousand dollars a month through our bank, but he can't manage his money well enough to pay back his loan."

"I'd like to talk with Dr. McPhearson. Have him give me a call," I suggested.

In late March 1981, the call came. "Hi, Carol. This is Phil Mcphearson. Did Lonnie tell you I was going to be getting in touch with you?"

"Yes, he did. He told me a little bit about you and your business."

"I'd like to sit down with you sometime and discuss a possible working relationship."

"When would you like to get together?"

"The sooner the better for me."

"Would tomorrow be soon enough?"

The following day, I was at Dr. McPhearson's office at three P.M. sharp.

"Hello, Carol. Good to see you. Please come in." Dr. McPhearson and I talked in generalities for an hour, about my experience and his clinic. Finally, he asked, "What will it take for you to come to work for me, Carol?"

"Dr. McPhearson, I'll come to work for you and run your clinic if you'll pay me twenty-five dollars for each abortion we do." If Chuck could pay me twenty-five dollars for each referral, Dr. McPhearson could surely pay me the same to run his clinic. Then I added, "And I'm looking for an equity opportunity as well."

"Carol, I'm not prepared to offer you twenty-five dollars per abortion or an equity position. However, I am willing to pay you two thousand dollars a month to run my clinic."

I considered his offer. "When would you want me to start?"

"Monday."

I had an ace in the hole. I was going to give Harvey Johnson one last chance to join forces with me. I couldn't wait to get to his clinic and tell him about the offer.

"Harvey, Phil McPhearson has offered me a tremendous opportunity to go to work for him. Looks like you and I are going to be in competition. I don't want that, do you? If I'm going to work for someone, it might as well be you."

"Carol, you know I can't afford to pay you a salary," he said, "because we're operating on a shoestring here. I can pay you twenty-five dollars for each abortion we do. If you build the business, you can make a lot of money. We did forty abortions last month, but I know you can increase the numbers quickly. How do you feel about it?" His offer was what I'd hoped for.

It didn't take me long to compute how much money I could make: forty times twenty-five dollars equaled one thousand dollars—not bad for a part-time job. But, four hundred times twenty-five dollars equaled ten thousand dollars—not bad for a month's work.

I understood Harvey Johnson, and I knew I had to be careful in my dealings with him. He had to think he was coming out ahead. "Harvey, you know I can't live on a thousand dollars a month. I'll have to keep my other job and just work here on Wednesdays and Saturdays. I may not even be able to be here every Wednesday, but I can be here every Saturday. Would that work?"

"We'll make it work," he agreed. "I know you can build the business quickly. What do you say, Carol?" he asked, slipping his arm around my shoulder.

"You've got a deal. I'll be here Saturday morning." I left Harvey's office feeling ecstatic, but I realized Harvey only included me because he felt compelled—he and his free help couldn't build the business as he wanted. It was a business decision for him, nothing more.

But Carol was back in business, on track again toward her goal of becoming the leading lady in the abortion industry. Nothing else mattered to me, as long as I could see I was getting closer to the object of my aspirations.

Although Harvey didn't include Wayne in the clinic deal, he still used him as an adviser. Wayne told Harvey he'd made a bad deal with me. His advice at the time was almost prophetic: "Don't get in bed with Carol; it won't work." Harvey didn't listen, of course, and we were partners once again.

Clinic ownership was not discussed when Harvey hired me, but he knew I wanted to be more than an employee. In our new working arrangement, Harvey was the medical director and the only abortionist. I was in charge of marketing, running the front office, the laboratory, procedure and recovery areas, and all-round flunky—chief cook and bottle washer, as the saying goes.

I knew what it took to keep Harvey happy. I made him think he made every decision. He was my ticket to wealth and the security for my children's college education. *Eventually,* I reasoned, *Harvey will help me get where I want to go. It's only a matter of time until I have a part of this business. I need Harvey Johnson, and he needs me.*

I immediately began to make changes at the clinic. I trained our telephone counselors to use sales techniques instead of counseling techniques.

I put Kelly on the telephone in the afternoon. She was thoroughly trained in how to sell an abortion. I paid her well to bring in the clients and our numbers began to rise right away. However, there was one line Kelly would not cross, even for me: she wouldn't go to the back where the killing was done.

Barbara, Harvey's young medical assistant, had similar misgivings. Barbara didn't like abortions. She actually used a fetal development to show women how developed their babies were at various stages of pregnancy. I stopped that practice immediately. Although Barbara was a good employee, I let her know that if she could not sell abortions, she had to go. She left.

In April, my first partial month at the clinic, we did forty-five abortions; my first month's income was $1,125. At the end of the second month the total was sixty-five abortions; my part-time income was $1,625. In June we did eighty-nine abortions; my paycheck was $2,225.

Things looked good. Fate was smiling on me and my old pal, Harvey. We were once again set to "help" women—augmenting the ranks of the post-abortive women's society while we lined our pockets with gold.

We viewed ourselves as poor grubstakers who had to get our clinic up to speed with the competition, and fast. Furnishing a growing clinic takes money—unless you're Harvey Johnson. All I had to do was make up a list of what I needed and give it to Harvey.

"Here's the list of supplies we need. We need the sterilization wrap before you come back on Saturday. Can you get it and send it over by Jan so I can have everything ready on Saturday?"

"I'm not on call before Saturday, and you know most of my supply trips are 'midnight requisition,'" he replied, "but I'll see what I can do. What about suture? Do we have any?"

"No, we don't. And we'd be in big trouble if we needed it."

"I'll be sure we get some. I think we've been getting the pregnancy tests from my office, right?"

"Harvey, I don't know where you get them from. I only know I give you the list and you bring supplies back from somewhere," I said.

"Pretty soon we're going to have to start buying our supplies. Someone is going to catch me," he winked.

"I'll start doing some price checks, then. I think I can find some deals. You know, we'd only have to pay twenty-one cents for each pregnancy test if we buy them directly from Neal. Your clinic is probably paying about fifty cents for the same test."

Harvey brought me whatever I needed from Garland Memorial Hospital and from his Garland partnership and continued to do so until we reached the monthly mark of two hundred abortions.

I had a tiny advertising budget because of limited funds. Dr. Robinson, the previous owner, had taken out a small *Yellow Pages* ad which wasn't generating much business. I had to come up with some creative, inexpensive advertising methods.

I found some coupon advertisers who were willing to run abortion-clinic ads. We placed ads offering a ten percent discount if the woman brought the coupon with her. It worked.

We also placed discount coupon ads in the *Dallas Times Herald* and the *Dallas Morning News TV Guide* section, using the coupons to track our results. The ads continued to work. Harvey joked, "One day, someone is going to gather up our coupons and bring them all in. We're going to have to pay her to do her abortion."

We were like one big happy family. Kelly, my daughter, and Jan, Harvey's daughter, handled the telephones. Both girls were still in high school but had been well trained in telephone counseling. In addition, they did lab work, in-house counseling, staffed the recovery room, and washed and sterilized instruments when necessary. Fredi, Harvey's live-in girlfriend, kept the books and worked the front office. We continued using Harvey's office staff from Garland as back-up.

A Man Like Harvey

My confidence in Harvey was at an all-time high. Things were going splendidly, both in the clinic and in my working relationship with him. He was sleeping with Fredi but that was fine with me—I was working my own agenda with him.

Harvey was well established in the Dallas/Garland medical community and had no problem sharing our association with the world. His open attitude with his peers increased my confidence in our relationship.

With a sensual man like Harvey and a woman like me, the sexual overtones were always there—but not acted upon. Sexual energy was always an undercurrent in our relationship, at least on my part. But I managed to control it.

Harvey was my constant telephone companion; we talked at least three times a day. He checked in with me when he got to his Garland office in the morning. "Good morning, Carol. How many do you have scheduled for today?"

"We'll have a pretty full day."

"That's good. Talk to you later. Love you."

"I love you, too."

The phrase "I love you" peppered our conversation. I could pour my love out on him as long as Fredi wasn't around. He usually called again in the middle of the afternoon, and once more at about nine o'clock to say "good night." I'll admit it: I was addicted to his phone calls.

Harvey wasn't good with my children. He was jealous of Joe Bob (as Tom had been) and loved Kelly (as Tom had not). For her part, Kelly really responded to the attention he gave her.

It's no surprise that as close as Harvey and I were, Fredi and I did not get along. In fact, we were on a collision course. I wanted Fredi to stay at home and out of the clinic, but Fredi knew what happened when Harvey's woman stayed out of his business. She herself had started dating Harvey before his marriage to Phyllis, his second wife.

Harvey could do better, I thought, *he could have me*. Oddly, that thought scared me to death. For the first time, I let myself think about my deepest feelings toward Harvey Johnson. Deep down, I wanted more than just a professional relationship with him. Jealousy, that old green-eyed spider that lived inside of me, was spreading its web to entangle my relationship with Fredi. Realizing the danger, I tried to pull myself back together and go to work.

Fredi didn't understand how the clinic worked, but she surely did understand me and how *I* worked. Once I asked her, "How many patients are in today?"

"Are you figuring how much money you're going to make?" Fredi asked, sarcastically.

Keeping my temper under control, I replied, "I have to keep the instruments sterilized and the rooms ready. The patient count has a bearing on how I do that." But I was thinking, *What an idiot. Yes, I'm figuring how much money I'm making, but I do have other responsibilities.*

The problem was that Fredi and I were very much alike—both headstrong, independent, and controlling. It was a constant battle of wills.

For his part, Harvey thrived on working all of us against each other. He used Jan Batson, his Garland office nurse, against me, Fredi against me, me against them all, and so on. He was a master at this sort of manipulation and enjoyed it very much. Part of my fun was laughing with him about what he was doing with all of us.

Harvey Johnson was no dummy. He knew exactly how to work each one of us, especially me. He knew I wanted to make a lot of money and operate my own clinic.

A Promised Partnership—Finally

We were sitting in Harvey's office one day, using a table for a desk, when he said, "Carol, we can run the abortion clinic without anybody else's help if we have to. Fredi can run the front; you can do the back and oversee everything. I can do the abortions. Our daughters can do lab and recovery. We don't need anybody else. We're a family. We're making good money already, and you're making a good living, too."

"But not as good as I want, Harvey. You know I want to make more money," I reminded him.

"All the corporate money goes right back into the clinic for expansion," he answered. "No one is taking anything out except your fee and the abortion fee for me. I live on that."

"I want to be more than an employee, Harvey."

"You are more than an employee. You, Fredi, and I are in this together. We're going to build this business and then issue stock. We're a family."

"You keep saying I'm more than an employee, Harvey, but nothing's been done about it."

"I've been thinking about it, Carol, and I'm ready to do something. The corporation papers haven't been changed since I took over the clinic from Dr. Robinson. We need to get that taken care of. I've thought about it, and I've decided to be the president; you'll be the vice president; Fredi will be the secretary-treasurer. Can you take the papers to Dr. Robinson's lawyer in Duncanville and have him draw up the necessary documents?"

"I'll call him this afternoon." I wanted to dance to the music he was making. I wanted to shout, but I contained myself.

Not that there wasn't a sore spot in what he told me. Although I didn't say anything, Harvey knew I didn't want Fredi in on the deal. A promised one-third interest in the business was better than what I'd had. He continued: "I'm ready to move on. Let's get this done and get on with making this business grow." *And making me rich,* I thought.

When the papers were prepared, the lawyers called. The new corporation was Dallas Medical Ladies Clinic, Inc. The papers were signed, and I proudly made out the checks for the incorporation fees to the State of Texas.

When the papers came back from the state, it was business as usual at the office, but it was celebration inside for me. I'd finally done it! Carol Nan Everett finally was the star of her own show—a small play with a lot of potential. Now was the time to really go to work. No more part-time stuff for me.

I began to pour all of my time into the clinic. We had to increase our advertising. I went to Harvey and asked, "What do you think about assuming the half-page ad I placed in the *Yellow Pages* before I left Chuck?"

"What do you mean, Carol?"

"We can probably take over that ad and pay a mileage fee."

"Okay. Check and see what it'll cost."

In September, the first month, the ad paid for itself.

"How many abortions did we do, Harvey?" I said with a smile, knowing it had been a good month.

"We did two hundred. I wonder if Chuck knows we're here now? I hope he's hurting."

"I'll bet he is," I chimed in. "I wonder how many abortions we missed that Chuck got from that *Yellow Pages* ad?" (Our Abortion Advisory Clinic ad was the number just before Chuck's Abortion Advisory Services ad.) At the time, I never understood why Harvey was so interested in hurting Chuck, but if it made Harvey happy, I wanted to hurt Chuck, too. Every problem of his that we knew about, every chance we had to discredit him, we utilized to the fullest.

My personal goal when I started working with Harvey in April 1981 was to reach two hundred abortions per month by December and five thousand dollars in personal income per month. I hit my goal in just six months.

"Carol, you're really making good money."

"Not good enough yet, Harvey. I have some big goals. You know I'm going to have two children in college soon, and you know how much that costs."

I already had my sights set on my next six-month goal—four hundred abortions and ten thousand dollars a month in take-home pay by the end of March, 1982. When I got there, I planned to reward myself with a new Oldsmobile Toronado.

I began to push Harvey on two fronts. "Harvey, we need to increase our abortion days and hire some doctors to help you."

"Okay, Carol. I'll get someone to help me so we can do abortions six days a week."

"And…we need to start doing second-trimester abortions. We can really increase our business if we start doing bigger ones."

"Up to how many weeks, Carol?"

"At least up to twenty weeks, don't you think?" I was suggesting that we terminate pregnancies in the fifth month.

"Let me think about it," he said.

The next Wednesday when Harvey came in, he said, "Start scheduling up to twenty weeks."

Even though it was harder on the patients, Harvey started doing a one-day, traumatic dilation abortion up to twenty weeks into the pregnancy. We were the only clinic I knew of doing that kind of procedure in one day. Within a few weeks, Harvey found other abortionists to help us so we could expand operations to six days a week.

The business rolled in. My goal for March, 1982 looked to be within reach. Harvey was doing just fine, helping me get where I wanted to go. But I still wasn't satisfied. We had to do more abortions, and even bigger ones.

"Harvey, everything has gone really well with our doing twenty-week abortions. What do you think about going to twenty-four weeks?" This would be six months into a pregnancy. "It'll increase our business—and our revenue—significantly. What do you think?"

"Let's do it to twenty-three weeks, Carol. That'll give us a one-week margin of error."

The ambition inside me to have top billing in the abortion industry drove me to push Harvey into doing bigger and bigger abortions. The recognition and reward were waiting for me, almost in my grasp. I was nearly where I wanted to be.

9

COMPLICATIONS & COVER-UPS

THE SCENE of Sheryl Mason lying in a pool of blood in the recovery room became etched in my mind. Her blood could be washed off the privacy curtains, the wall, and the bedding, but it could never be washed off me.

Sheryl Mason walked into our "clean" clinic, and we killed her. My soul languished in a mire of blame. *"I'm as guilty as Harvey, because I sold her the abortion, and I pushed him into doing big abortions. I'm covered with Sheryl's blood. I'm the Scarlet Lady.*

Carrying the responsibility for Sheryl's death became another endurance test for me. From the time I began the push toward bigger abortions, I became disappointed in our performance as a "professional" operation.

But I forced myself to accept that we weren't the perfect clinic I'd imagined we were. I came to adopt Harvey's rationale: "Our number was just up; we can't worry about it." I had concentrated on selling abortions and had continued to push Harvey to do more big ones. Why couldn't I see what was coming?

Less than a month after Sheryl's death, we transported Laura in my car—not to the closest hospital nor to the hospital that would take the best care of her, but to a hospital that would cover for us, Garland Memorial, where Dr. Harvey Johnson was chief of staff.

Laura, a twenty-five-year-old referred to us by a doctor in Garland, was admitted to Garland Memorial for a hysterectomy. She was diagnosed as having *placenta previa*—the placenta being presented in the mouth of the uterus. Harvey once again rationalized, "If she had gone full-term, the results would have been the same."

Having gone through the ordeal of Sheryl's death, I was much stronger now and more calloused. Laura's hysterectomy was a minor glitch, nothing more.

The abortion business, like all other businesses, has its cycles. January is a good month; February is okay. March is great, April tops, May good, and the summer back to merely okay. At the end of August, just before school starts, things really pick up. September is dynamite, October shaky; November and December are good. But in our case, each month, the business increased.

Our *Yellow Pages* advertising, plus our discount coupon promotions, continued to pay big dividends. Our contacts with "do-gooder" agencies yielded a stream of good referrals. The increased abortion days, using more abortionists, and doing bigger abortions kept our business humming. We started getting referrals from other abortion clinics because of our one-day, second-trimester procedure.

And of course, we were beginning to get repeat clients. They began to refer their friends and bring in their sisters because of the good job we did for them the first time.

By March we were back on track, and I believed my ten thousand dollars a month in income was a safe bet. On March 2, 1982, I rewarded myself and bought my new Toronado, as planned. Harvey gave the dealership a statement saying I had earned seventy thousand dollars in 1981.

Even Harvey seemed to be impressed with my new success. "Carol, you're really making good money."

"Not enough, Harvey," continued to be my answer. I'm sure Harvey was thrilled to hear that; it meant more money for him, too. I was driven by an insatiable desire to make more money.

Personal Costs

The new car smell was still fresh in my Toronado when Dr. Burney, one of the doctors Harvey had recruited to allow us to expand our services, botched Lisa's abortion. At the same time, Dr. Johnson botched the abortion of a twenty-seven-year-old from a small town in Arkansas.

The past five months had seen too many botched abortions. We were maiming at least one woman a month; one out of every five hundred had to have major surgery.

Lisa was a twenty-one-year-old single mother with a two-year-old child. She was twenty weeks pregnant.

Dr. Burney did her abortion, which proceeded uneventfully until he said to me, "Carol, she has a polyp on the back of her uterus, and I think I'll pull it off."

He pulled and pulled, but he couldn't get it off.

He called Dr. Johnson from across the hall, where he was doing abortions. "Harvey, I think this woman has a polyp on the back of her uterus. I've tried to pull it off, but I can't. Could you help me?"

"Yes," Harvey replied.

Both doctors pulled and pulled, but they couldn't get the polyp out. They finally gave up and sent Lisa to recovery. I believe they pulled Lisa's uterus wrong-side-out.

Her vital signs became erratic. At about four o'clock, Dr. Johnson called me to the recovery room with that now-familiar sick look on his face. "Carol, Lisa is hemorrhaging. We're going to have to take her to the hospital. I've called Garland Memorial. We have a room scheduled for surgery at five o'clock. Pull your car around, and I'll drive."

Harvey was angry that he was having to cover for Dr. Burney's botched abortion, but we both knew we had to protect the clinic.

What will happen to Lisa? I wondered. *She'll have a hysterectomy now, so she can't have any more children. She'll miss at least a month's work. How will she and her two-year-old live?*

When I saw Lisa six weeks later, she had changed from a thin and beautiful woman to an overweight woman whose eyes had lost their sparkle.

Another patient, the woman from Arkansas, came in with her parents. She thought she was about twenty weeks pregnant. Dr. Johnson, who examined her, determined he could do the abortion.

Using local anesthesia and a small dosage of Valium, Harvey started the abortion, but discovered the baby was too far advanced. Its muscle structure was so strong that its body wouldn't come apart. After almost an hour on the table, with six nurses holding the woman and pulling her away from Harvey, the baby's body finally separated from the head. Then Harvey worked and worked to crush the head and remove it. It was a very long ordeal for both the woman and Dr. Johnson.

One of the nurses, Becky, who usually never reacted to anything, rolled her eyes back in her head. I thought for a minute she was going to faint.

After the procedure, Harvey measured the baby's foot. He tried to hide the measurement from me, but I saw it—the baby was about thirty-two weeks along, probably old enough to survive outside its mother.

The baby's body was too large to go down the garbage disposal, so Harvey suggested I take it to our competitor's trash receptacle, so that if it were found, it would be in their trash, not ours. Dutifully, I wrapped the baby in a paper drape, put it in a brown paper sack, and planted it, after dark, in the other clinic's trash.

Harvey had to hospitalize the woman. His dismissal diagnosis: some sort of heart problem.

Insanely, I kept pushing to do more abortions and "bigger" ones. I was hopelessly hooked by the love of money and what it could do for me next. After remodeling my home, I planned to buy two new sports cars for the children. I was consumed with the thought of all the things I was going to do...and blithely forgetful of the horrors we were committing at the clinic.

Ironically, I began tithing again when I went into business with Harvey. God had answered my prayer for success, I thought. Now I believed I was right where God wanted me—helping women.

I kept a Bible in my top right-hand drawer and pulled it out if someone said, "Abortion is a sin." My answer was emphatic: "I am helping women because God wants me to. I tithe out of all the money I make. I pray every day." It was true, but I didn't tell them I actually prayed for freedom from complications and deaths, and for more abortions every day.

When I went to church in San Saba, all the deacons were so nice to me. Many of them never noticed me before I started sending my tithe back to the church. The minister was always very nice, and when a new minister came, he immediately knew who I was. One of the deacons asked my father, "Does she tithe at a Dallas church, too?"

"Probably so," Daddy bragged.

Everyone in the church paid special attention when I visited. They knew I had donated two pews, one in memory of my sister and the other in memory of my grandfather. My grandmother attended the church and was very proud of me. She moved from her regular seat to sit in the new pew I had given in my grandfather's honor.

Money can do a lot for you, even in God's house and among God's people. I used it to buy their approval.

I even believed God was blessing me in the abortion industry because of my tithe. If I stopped tithing, I reasoned, God would stop blessing me financially. The first check I wrote after receiving my pay was to the church, and I did it without fail. I was afraid to forget "His" check, for fear that the financial goodies surely would stop—and I didn't want that to happen.

I believed God was answering my prayers and honoring my tithe. More women were coming for abortions, despite Sheryl's death and the botched procedures.

I was reveling in my new role in May 1982, when Jenni danced into the clinic. Why did she have to be so arrestingly easy to remember? Why did she have to be so close to Kelly's age? Jenni's tragedy came to haunt me more than all the others.

Jenni was beautiful; she was tall and stylishly thin, with brunette hair. At the age of twenty-one, she loved attention and knew how to get it—with her body. That was obvious the moment she entered the clinic that Wednesday afternoon.

I took her back to the examining room for her pregnancy to be sized by a doctor before she paid for the procedure. "Take your clothes off from the waist down, and have a seat on the edge of the table," I directed.

Unashamed, she raised her multi-colored sun-dress to reveal she was wearing no underwear, hopped up on the table, and lay down. I draped her with a sheet, opened the door, and told Harvey, "We're ready."

Harvey came in, patted Jenni on the leg, and said with a reassuring smile, "Hi, baby. We're just going to check you to see how big you are. It won't hurt."

I handed him the glove, squeezed the K-Y Jelly out for him, and watched him proceed with the examination.

"It looks like you're twenty-two weeks along," Harvey commented as he finished the examination. "The pelvic is normal, so the procedure can be done without any problem. The fee will be seven hundred and fifty dollars if we put you to sleep, and it will be easier on you if we do. Do you have the money?" Harvey removed the glove and tossed it into the wastebasket.

"Yes, and I have enough to be put to sleep," Jenni replied, "seven hundred and fifty dollars. Connie said it's much easier if I can afford to be put to sleep. I hate pain. I have a fifteen-month-old daughter living in Nevada with my parents. Her birth nearly killed me. I just can't stand pain." Jenni spoke quickly, her voice sounding young and carefree.

"Yes, Jenni, it would be much easier on you. I'll be in the room with you. Everything is going to be all right," I assured her.

Harvey patted her on the leg again. "I'll see you later," he promised.

"Let's go up to the front desk, so you can pay," I continued. "Have a seat there, and you'll be called soon."

I went to check out the operating room to be sure it was ready. The instruments had to be prepared: large dilators—sterilized, yet cool enough to handle; a number sixteen cannula—a tube to insert into the uterus; and Bierhoff forceps, to remove the pieces of the unwanted baby.

It took a little while for us to get everything ready. I checked on Jenni several times to make sure she was okay, that she wasn't getting too nervous. "Where do you work, Jenni?" I asked.

"I work at a local Ford dealership," she answered, flipping through the pages of an old magazine.

"And where do you live?"

"With my grandparents."

I knew, even without her admission, that she had run away from problems back in Nevada. We discussed her daughter, who was living with her parents. Jenni didn't seem to miss her, although she talked about her; it was as though the child were a part of her history, but not a part of her. She talked to me about several of her lovers, but never about the father of her child.

"Jenni, everything's ready now," I called. "This won't take long."

"I don't have on any underwear," she announced as she danced into the operating room, pulling up her dress for all to see. "Let's get it over with." She jumped up on the table and waited for us to give her a sheet.

The other nurses watched in amazement. I had seen similar acts before: Jenni was scared, and trying very hard not to show it.

After the anesthetist put her to sleep, I placed my hand on Jenni's abdomen. I felt movement, one of the only babies I can remember moving inside the mother during an abortion.

Harvey proceeded as normal: He cleaned off her cervix with Betadine, dilated her, and suctioned briefly to break the bag of amniotic fluid surrounding the baby. The baby didn't move after he finished suctioning. The next step required Harvey to crush the baby inside Jenni's uterus and then remove its body piece by piece, using the Bierhoff forceps.

The first time Harvey reached in, he pulled out placental tissue. The second time he reached in, he pulled out the lining around the colon. Immediately, I saw the shock on Harvey's face. I couldn't see what he had pulled out, but the look on his face told me it was serious.

His face was ashen as he spoke. "It's over. I pulled out omentum"—the term for the viscera connecting the abdominal structures. He frantically tried to push the bowel back into the uterine cavity, but to no avail. "We have to take her to the hospital, Carol."

"It can't be over!" I objected. "The baby isn't even dead. It's still intact. We can't take this woman to the hospital with a live baby still inside her! It can't be over! Surely there's something we can do." I knew my voice sounded hysterical, but I couldn't believe this was happening.

"No, Carol, there isn't anything." Harvey pushed back from the table. He leaned toward me, looking dejected, and said quietly, "We have to take her to the hospital."

Harvey knew he had blown this one badly. He was scared to death, and it showed.

"Where will we take her?" I asked. Garland Memorial was out of the question; lately we had taken too many botched abortions there. Dr. George was now checking every one of Harvey's charts, trying to catch one of his travesties.

Harvey stood up, picked up the pan for the body parts, and walked out of the room. I followed him into Central Supply where he slowly removed his gloves. I silently waited for his decision.

As we headed to his office, he said, "I'm going to call Lloyd. He'll help us."

Harvey always seemed to have a list of people who owed him a favor. He called them in at times like this.

My mind raced ahead, clicking off what I knew of the medical procedures. *If her bowel has come out through the vagina, the uterus has to be perforated. With the baby alive and a bowel resection needed, this will be quite a surgical procedure, requiring several specialists. Harvey can't do the bowel resection. And what will they do with the baby's body in a hospital?*

I had things to do. I hurried to the front desk to tell the staff I would be gone for a while. Something in me wanted my daughter Kelly with me at the hospital. I needed someone to go with me, but the twisted truth is I wanted her to experience the ordeal of taking a woman to the hospital. She had to be trained and tested, I reasoned. She had to know how to do whatever was required.

"Kelly, we have a problem in the back. I have to take someone to the hospital, and I want you to go with me to hold the IV bag. Please take my keys and move my car to the back door of the recovery room, and be ready to go." Of course, we had to use my car; an ambulance is terrible publicity in front of an abortion clinic.

"What's wrong?" she asked. I could see Kelly trying to read the answer in my expression.

"Jenni has a problem. I don't know all the details, but we have to go. Come on. Move the car, baby," I pleaded.

By now, supervisors and employees were becoming accustomed to the quietly frantic relocation of a botched abortion to a hospital. They ignored us as best they could.

I checked again with Harvey to be sure everything was set with Lloyd. "What are we going to do?" I asked him.

"Let me... Let me think about this," he mumbled.

Harvey made some more telephone calls and then finally said, "Move her to your car, and take her to Garland Humana Hospital. They've been trying to get me to use their hospital. Take her to the emergency room entrance, and Dr. Lloyd will meet you there."

He dropped his hand on my shoulder and looked directly into my eyes. "Do *not* tell anyone what happened. I told Lloyd I was taking care of another doctor's problems. Don't even mention my name," he emphasized.

"Don't worry; I won't." I hurried to the back.

"Leslie, put Jenni into my car."

Leslie had helped me move women before, so she knew exactly what to do. She moved the wheelchair next to the operating table and locked the brakes in place.

"Jenni, can you sit up? We're going to move you now."

"Is it over, Carol?" she mumbled.

"Jenni, there's been a problem. We have to move you to the hospital for additional surgery. We can't do it in the clinic." I was calm and matter-of-fact.

"I can't go to the hospital. I don't have any insurance."

"We have to take you to the hospital. You must be treated. We can't stop now."

"What about money?"

"Jenni, I can't answer you. Help us get you into the wheelchair and out to the car. Is there anyone you would like for us to call to have with you at the hospital?"

"Yes. Call Sharon. Tell her what's happened. See if she can come to the hospital." As we wheeled Jenni out the back door, she asked, "Are you taking me to the hospital in a car?" She sounded confused.

I took over. "Yes, and Kelly is going to ride with us. Leslie and I will lift your arms while you stand up. I hope it doesn't hurt, but we have to move you to the car."

Kelly held the IV, her eyes wide. She had never seen anything like this.

I started snapping out orders. "Jenni, I'm going to recline that seat as far as I can. Kelly, I'll hold the IV while you go around and get in the back seat." Obediently, Kelly hurried around the car and got in. "Here, Kelly, hold it up over her head. Keep it running."

"Which hospital are we going to?" Jenni wanted to know.

"Garland Humana."

"I've never heard of it. Where is it?"

"It's a good hospital in Garland. My son had an operation there."

"It hurts. Where's Dr. Johnson?"

"He'll meet us at the hospital."

"How much longer? I can't stand the pain. Hurry! Why is it taking so long?"

"We're going to a good hospital with the best doctors. It's in Garland and it takes a little longer to get there. You'll be well cared for. It'll only be a few more minutes." I tried to keep as calm as possible, much calmer than I actually felt.

Jenni screamed in pain all the way to the hospital. Every time I looked at my daughter, I wished I hadn't brought her. Kelly was scared, nervous, and stunned.

For some time I had wanted Kelly's validation of abortion and my part in it, but she had been noncommittal. I felt she was acting the part of a pro-choice supporter just to win my approval.

If Kelly was going to be good in the business, she had to learn it all. I had recently forced her to watch a big procedure, her first one. She didn't like it at all; she kept trying to get out of the room. I insisted she stay through the entire procedure, however, and afterward she was very upset, refusing to talk to me about it.

Now this plan was backfiring on me, too. Kelly seemed to be putting herself in Jenni's place. She didn't seem at all confident about what her mother was doing.

Riding to the hospital, I, too, began to identify Jenni with Kelly. *This could be Kelly in trouble. How would I feel if this were happening to my daughter?* I didn't like the answer.

"Kelly, how's that IV doing?" Back to reality.

"It's still running."

"Good. Thank you, baby, for helping me." I concentrated on driving and was very relieved when the entrance to Garland Humana appeared ahead.

"Jenni, here we are. Let's find the Emergency Room. There it is." I pulled into the parking spot reserved for ambulances and jumped out of the car. "Kelly, I'm going in to get a stretcher. Stay in the car."

A nurse stepped out into the hall as I entered. "May I help you?"

"Yes. I have an emergency admission in the car. We need a gurney."

"Does the patient have a doctor?" she asked as she rounded a corner to get the stretcher.

"Yes, Dr. Lloyd is supposed to meet us here."

An angry Dr. Lloyd came out of nowhere. "Carol, come here. I'll tell you right now, I'm *not* covering for Harvey this time!"

The nurse returned with a gurney and Jenni was quickly moved to a room. Suddenly the nurse yelled, "There's pitocin in the IV! Is she an abortion patient?"

Jenni screamed, "Where is Dr. Johnson?"

"Did Harvey do her abortion, Carol?" Dr. Lloyd questioned.

Before I could answer, Harvey walked up, slipped his arm over Dr. Lloyd's shoulder, and the two walked toward Jenni's emergency room. Dr. Lloyd was arguing, but I could tell Harvey would win him over, as usual.

I hugged Kelly and sent her back to the clinic in my car.

We've Got to Protect the Clinic

Harvey reappeared briefly to direct me to the doctor's lounge to wait while Jenni's surgery was performed. I went through hell in that room while I waited on Harvey. Painful as it was to admit, I knew we were not helping women have safe abortions; instead, we were maiming and even killing them. How had this happened?

Why did it bother me so much—so suddenly? Why was Jenni's botched abortion making me question my future in the abortion industry?

I finally decided it had to do with the look in Kelly's eyes—how she stared at me in the rear view mirror as we drove Jenni to the hospital; the way she looked at me at the hospital when she said, "I want to go; I want to go back to the office." She had looked right through me. What was it about that look?

Suddenly, all of my efforts to convince Kelly we were helping women were revealed for the lies they were—lies to justify myself—and Kelly knew. Kelly saw more than she needed to see. I made a big mistake in having her go with me to the hospital.

Fear of Kelly's rejection engulfed me. *My baby is going to reject me! I know she sees even more inside me. Can she see I'm one of them—a member of the post-abortive women's society?*

Kelly sees me covering up botched abortions. She knows I'm a hypocrite. She knows abortions hurt, especially botched ones. She knows the pain of a botched abortion vicariously, having suffered with Jenni and feeling her every scream.

Kelly is just two years younger than Jenni. She must be thinking, "That could be me." I'm sure she thinks, "My mother did this; she's in charge. This is my mother—a butcher."

I'm really scared. I'm going to lose Kelly, my baby. Who will I have when she's gone? Doesn't she realize how much I need her?

I came to a startling revelation: I was not as upset about what happened to Jenni as I was about how Kelly felt toward me.

I accepted the revelation. When you take the leading role, you have to be prepared to pay a high price. Nothing—not Harvey, not Sheryl's death, not my kids—nothing is going to stop me from achieving my goals.

Hell and pain are a part of success. So what if you walk over a few people to win, bend the rules a little? Kelly will be okay. I've just got to work harder to win her over. She'll come around. Somehow I'll make it up to her for what I put her through.

That's what I tried to tell myself, but it didn't ring true. The more I reflected on our botched abortions, the sicker I felt. All of our doctors were bungling abortions, but Harvey—my beloved, trusted Harvey— had the worst record. Yes, he did perform most of the big abortions. But the other doctors handled these cases without as high a complication rate as Harvey had.

What am I going to do about Harvey messing up so many abortions? I wondered. Harvey was very important—the medical director of the clinic. He was the one we needed when a major complication occurred; his help was vital in all facets of the coverups. I also needed Harvey personally; he was such an important part of my support system. *What am I going to do? And how can I keep my plans a secret from Harvey as long as Fredi is in the clinic?*

I forced my attention to the problem at hand. *I just know the legal forces are going to come out of the woodwork this time. We've really blown it. We're going to be sued for everything we ever dreamed of owning—and we deserve it!*

Get hold of yourself, Carol. Go check to see if Jenni's friend is here. Find out if she's friend or foe.

I left the doctor's lounge and found the surgery waiting room. A pretty blonde woman in her early twenties was nervously sitting on the edge of the couch. "Are you a friend of Jenni Richardson?" I asked.

"Yes," she replied. "Who are you?" I motioned for her to stay seated and I joined her on the adjacent couch.

"I'm Carol Everett, from the clinic. Jenni's in surgery and will be out soon, but she'll be in the recovery room for a time before she goes to her room. How well do you know Jenni?" I kept my voice level.

"I met her at work, and we've been out together several times," she responded.

"Are you close to her?"

"Are you asking me if I knew why she was at the clinic?"

"Yes, I suppose I am," I admitted.

"I know she was having an abortion today, and she had mixed emotions about it. She was scared, but happy it was about to be over," she said.

"Do you know her family?"

"Jenni lives with her grandparents in Plano, and her parents live in Nevada. I don't think she gets along with her grandparents. They have some old-fashioned ideas. I've never met them, but I did telephone them a little while ago."

"Are they coming to the hospital?" I asked.

"Not today."

"Did they know Jenni was having an abortion?"

"I'm not sure. They do wonder what happened, but I don't know what Jenni told them," she answered honestly. "How long do you think it will be before I can see Jenni?"

"I really don't know," I said, "but it'll be at least a couple of hours before she's back in her room, and she'll be groggy then. Are you going to wait?"

"I don't think so. I'll call back later tonight." The young woman stood up.

"I'll talk to Jenni tomorrow," I said. I'll tell her you were here. What's your name?"

"Sharon Clark." She extended her hand to me, which I clasped with relief.

"It's nice to meet you, Sharon. I'll see you later."

"Goodbye." And she headed toward the elevator.

Looks like we're safe with her friend and family.

I went back to the doctors' lounge. The waiting seemed like an eternity. A million thoughts ran through my mind—my daughter Kelly, Jenni, Harvey, botched abortions, the business. Finally, Harvey appeared in the door, looking haggard. "Carol, we don't have a problem anymore."

I couldn't believe my ears. How could we not have a problem? We had really blown it on Jenni. I assumed we could be facing a major lawsuit here.

"I'll tell you about it later," Harvey said. "Let's get out of here. Did any of her family come?"

"Only a friend, and she left."

As we walked out of the hospital, I realized I didn't feel the usual pride, walking with Harvey.

Harvey's Facade Begins to Crack

We drove to Harvey's house to pick up Fredi before they drove me home. On the way, he commented, "I have to talk to Dale, the pathologist, in the morning to work out a few things, but I'm sure the abdominal pregnancy was the cause of the colostomy."

I kept my mouth shut, but I certainly talked to myself.

Abdominal pregnancy? That was not an abdominal pregnancy. You examined her before the abortion. You would surely have picked that up in a physical examination of a five-and-a-half-month pregnancy. No competent doctor would have started an abortion on a woman with an advanced abdominal pregnancy.

So, this is how you choose to cover up this one! Have all of the doctors who operated with you agreed to write up the records as an abdominal pregnancy? Will the pathologist write up his records the same way? You're going to lie to keep us from being sued, and all of your doctor buddies are going to support your lie.

I couldn't stand it any longer. "Harvey, we've just ruined a young woman's body and her life. Jenni has had a colostomy. What if she were one of our children? What if she were Kelly, or your daughter, Jan? How would we feel?"

Harvey ignored my question. He calmly continued with the details of the surgical procedure. "I wrapped the baby in a disposable sheet and threw it with the trash in the surgical suite. No one will think it's anything other than a disposable sheet."

You really covered your tracks, I thought.

"Lloyd thinks he can resection the colostomy in about six months, so the colostomy will not be permanent," he told me.

"Thank heaven for that. Jenni is such a beautiful woman."

"The hospital administrator at Humana has been trying to get me to move my surgery over there for some time. I'll go see him in the morning. Maybe I can get him to write off the bill," Harvey added.

"Do you think he will?" I asked.

"They need the business, and I'll do a few cases over there if they do."

We pulled up to Harvey's house and Fredi joined us. "How did it go?" she asked when she got into the car.

"Everything is all right," he answered. "She had to have a

colostomy, but Dr. Smith checked her urinary tract, and everything is okay. It was an abdominal pregnancy."

I screamed inside. *He's lying to us, Fredi and me, the people who protect him from anything and everything. He can't even tell us the truth, that he blew it.*

I couldn't stand it. I had to let Harvey know I knew he was lying. My hand had been on that baby, and it was perfectly in place inside her uterus.

"Are you going to change the records at the clinic to reflect an abdominal pregnancy?" I asked, manipulatively.

"Do you mean it wasn't an abdominal pregnancy?" Fredi shot back, looking first at me, then at Harvey.

On the hot seat, Harvey did not answer directly, but said tersely to me, "You'll need to pull that chart and keep it in your office. I'll make some notes about the surgical procedure the next time I'm in the clinic."

"Harvey, what happened?" Fredi demanded.

"Everything is all right, Fredi. Jenni had an abdominal pregnancy, that's all. It's always critical when we hospitalize a patient from the clinic—you know that."

As we turned the corner of Marsh Lane and headed toward my house, I knew what I had to do about Harvey and his blown procedures. In the future, I would make sure Harvey Johnson did not do any abortion past fifteen weeks, which clearly seemed to be in his safety zone. I didn't know exactly how I was going to accomplish this without Fredi's knowledge, but Harvey Johnson was not going to do another big abortion if I could help it—and I could help it!

10

MAKING CHANGES,
COVERING TRACKS

I HAD OTHER DOCTORS who could safely do big abortions and, quite frankly, I wanted to reduce the pressure on Harvey by taking the big ones off his schedule. As I reflected on the events of the day, the cracks in Harvey's professional facade grew wider and wider.

The next morning, when Harvey made his regular call to check in, I asked about Jenni.

"Jenni's complaining about the pain, but she's fine this morning," he assured me. "She wants to know when she can go home. She asked about you, Carol. Call her soon."

He continued. "I went to pathology and talked to Dale. Everything is fine. Now—back to business. How many do you have scheduled today?"

"Nine," I responded.

"Have a good day, baby," he said, and he was off.

"You too, Harvey." I hung up, but my thoughts stayed on the line. *How superficial we are, while women are being needlessly maimed.*

As promised, I called Jenni. "Hi, Jenni. This is Carol from the clinic. How are you feeling today?"

"Terrible. I hurt all over. I don't understand why my back is hurting so much." She sounded extremely weak.

"You had some pretty extensive surgery," I explained. "An abdominal pregnancy affects your entire abdomen, and you'll be sore all over for a few days. Ask the nurse to give you something for the pain. I'm certain Dr. Johnson ordered something for you. Is there anything I can get you, Jenni?"

"Not now," she answered softly.

"Call me if you need anything, and I'll get it for you. Talk to you later. Goodbye."

I was very anxious to talk to Harvey that night for a complete update.

"I talked to the hospital administrator, and he agreed to write off Jenni's bill," he said. "I'll do a few cases at Garland Humana and hopefully, when the colostomy is reversed, he'll write off that bill, too. None of the other surgeons will send her a bill, so I think we'll be okay.

"When Jenni gets out of the hospital, I'll take her out a few times. And—Carol, you need to stay in touch with her. She likes you. Maybe you can take her to dinner a few times. I don't think Jenni will sue us if we take care of her."

I didn't share Harvey's enthusiasm for "befriending" this young woman to prevent a lawsuit, but I knew I'd do anything to keep this out of the news and reduce the legal risk. I privately wondered how many other women Harvey had dated to keep them from suing him.

Another crack in the facade. How long before it crumbles completely? I asked myself.

"How long will she be in the hospital?" I questioned Harvey.

"Lloyd will dismiss her—but probably no more than five to seven days," he estimated.

"How long before she can go back to work?"

"That depends on her, but…probably a month to six weeks."

"Looks like we have lots of baby-sitting ahead of us, then. You know, Jenni is just a little younger than our own kids, Jan and Joe Bob."

"Yeah, she's twenty-one years old… How was the day?" he asked, changing the subject.

"We did all nine procedures, but Leggett took three hours to do them. He talks too much. We have twenty-eight scheduled for tomorrow, and you know how Dr. Fisher moves. Also, Dr. Mosely is going to come by to do a big one on his lunch hour. He's inserted laminaria for two days, so the patient's cervix should be dilated sufficiently for the baby to come right out." I felt better, focusing on the clinic.

"Do we have a good weekend scheduled?" he asked.

"I don't remember how many are on for Saturday, but I know it's over thirty. June is starting off with some great numbers. We could have a really good month." I sounded more confident than I felt.

"Let's make it a good month. I'll talk to you in the morning. Love you, baby."

"I love you, too, Harvey. Good night."

What is "love," anyway? How often I've heard and said the words "I love you." I've discovered that frequently they're just so much wasted breath. I now realize it was that way with Harvey.

Playing the Game

After Jenni was released, she called me regularly at the clinic.

"Carol, I don't feel very pretty with this thing hanging out of my side," she said, referring to the colostomy bag.

I don't feel very pretty either with that thing hanging out of your side, Jenni, my heart answered, *but I have to play the game.* "It won't be long now, Jenni, before it can be removed," I told her. "Think of how pretty you'll look then."

I kept Harvey informed of all my contacts with Jenni.

Once, Jenni told me, "Dr. Johnson calls me all the time! He says he wants to take me to dinner. I'm very excited about seeing him." Knowing what I knew, it was hard to listen to the eagerness in her voice.

"I'm sure he'll call soon, Jenni," I said, hating every syllable. "I know he's looking forward to spending some time with you."

Jenni called me with more good news. "Dr. Johnson has asked me out to dinner! I'm so excited! I can hardly wait."

What could I say? I was sick to my stomach that Harvey would stoop so low—toying with the emotions of a scared, hurting, twenty-one-year-old, just to keep from being sued. Oh, I didn't want to be sued either, but I also didn't want to hurt Jenni any more than we already had.

At times I was tempted to tell her the truth so she *could* sue. *The facts will be out,* I reasoned, *and this whole masquerade will be over.* But I couldn't bring myself to betray Harvey.

"I'm excited for you, Jenni," I told her. "What are you going to wear?"

"I don't know…How do you think I should dress?" she asked eagerly.

"That sundress you wore to the clinic looks beautiful on you."

"Do you think it's dressy enough for an evening with Dr. Johnson?"

"Yes, I do. You'll have a great time. Let me know how it goes." I wondered what kind of time Harvey would have.

The date came and went. "We had a great time!" Jenni was thrilled to report. "I hope we can see each other regularly."

"You don't know how hectic a doctor's schedule is, Jenni," I cautioned. "I know he'll see you when he can." *I'm guilty, too. I'm playing with Jenni's emotions just like Harvey. I hate myself for this.*

As the time for the reversal of the colostomy drew near, Jenni called more and more. She was relieved that it was about to be over, but scared of the surgery and the pain.

"Carol, can you ask Dr. Lloyd to schedule me earlier?"

"Jenni, I can't tell the doctor what to do. You have to listen to him. He's the expert, and we don't want to rush him."

Harvey arranged for Dr. Lloyd to do the surgery free and for the hospital to write off both bills. Once again, he'd waved his magic wand.

Jenni called after the surgery, very excited. "Carol, I do have kind of a bad scar, but I don't have that bag! I can dance again!"

No lawsuit, my sweet Harvey. Jenni can dance again.

But I didn't know how many more dances I had left in me. Inside, I was sick of botched abortions…and sick of myself. Harvey was right again: "The business is going to be okay." But I wasn't so sure about me.

I began to reflect on my thirty-seven years of life and finally made these conclusions about Carol Nan Everett:

First, I was an unscrupulous woman who longed so much to be the top dog in the abortion industry that I would not hesitate to help cover up severely mishandled medical procedures—even to the point of falsifying medical records.

Second, I loved money and its privileges so much, I would continue to sell abortions, despite the potential consequences for the women involved.

The bottom line? I concluded that I would remain in the abortion business, and not only remain, but thrive. *A lot of work needs to be done if we are going to get our second clinic open by September and reach six hundred abortions by the end of the year,* I thought.

Despite my misgivings, the demon of greed had me in its grips. I wasn't about to quit, not now.

Professional Consequences

My attention shifted to Harvey. My confidence in him was so severely shaken by Jenni's botched abortion that I made the decision not only to take him off the late-term procedures, but also to stop using him as my personal physician.

Harvey's stupid mistakes could ruin my plans to be rich, I concluded. *The mistake with Jenni almost cost me my relationship with Kelly, too. That kind of thing cannot happen again.*

I knew Harvey had a tremendous battle going on inside him over doing big abortions. Maybe I'd pushed him too far. "The doctors at Garland Memorial are beginning to question my work," he once confided in me. Harvey needed my help, my loyalty, my protection—not my pushing. I decided it was best for him and the clinic to schedule him for first trimester abortions only.

I also began to distance myself personally from Harvey, and the clinic as well, from medical errors. The other doctors would have to take responsibility for their own mistakes.

But the mishandled abortions continued.

Dr. Burney did a procedure on a Mexican woman about thirty-two years old and approximately twenty weeks along. He perforated her uterus and the forceps severed her urinary tract. With her IV in place, I transferred her to Methodist Hospital in my car. Dr. Burney met me and admitted her. Her urinary tract was repaired surgically, and we saw the woman one more time for a checkup.

Dr. Mosely did an abortion on an eighteen-year-old who was eleven weeks pregnant. She screamed and screamed during the abortion, which was not normal. Dr. Mosely became very upset because the young woman would not stop screaming.

Billie, the nurse, kept telling the young woman, "Please be quiet, you are disturbing the other patients. You'll be fine."

She stopped screaming when the procedure was over and was discharged from recovery with no special care. Several days later, she called the clinic, complaining of discomfort. She was asked to come back in for a checkup, at which time we discovered her uterus had been perforated and her bowel pulled inside the uterus with the suction.

Dr. Mosely hospitalized her and had a surgeon do a colostomy. We divorced ourselves from that case quickly. "That's Mosely's problem, not ours," Harvey justified. "That's why the doctors are independent contractors and not paid by check." As if that made it better.

Dr. Miller handled cases on Monday night. During a procedure, he pushed the head of a fifteen-week-old baby into the mother's abdomen. "Carol, call Dr. Johnson. I have to admit her. She has to have surgery tonight."

I called Harvey and told him what Dr. Miller had done.

"Let me call Medical Arts to see if we can do the surgery there."

"Harvey will call back in a few minutes, Dr. Miller. Let's finish the other procedures."

Harvey called back. "Yes, take her to Medical Arts. I'll help Miller."

The next morning, as we walked out of the hospital, Harvey told me, "Miller was scared. I repaired her uterus and put the baby's head in a disposable sheet. I wrapped it tightly so no one would discover it. It was not a part of the specimen."

Still, Harvey and I concentrated our efforts on getting the Mockingbird office better prepared to support our second clinic. We had to get the second clinic open and operating very quickly in order to be doing six hundred abortions a month by the end of the year—and in order for my monthly income to increase to fifteen thousand dollars.

"Harvey, the central telephone bank will be the key to making us more successful than the other chains."

"I know, Carol. Get it set up."

I began to train our telephone counselors in preparation for future expansion. I also placed additional ads in the *Southwestern Bell Yellow Pages* with a single "800" number covering all of Texas, plus much of Louisiana, Oklahoma, Arkansas, and New Mexico. In preparation for choosing our second location, we had been doing some concentrated advertising in several potential areas and monitoring the results. Our plan called for us to build up to two hundred referrals in a key area, select a prime location in that area, secure a lease in a suitable facility, and open a clinic.

"It looks like the best location for our first satellite clinic is Mesquite. We're getting about two hundred referrals from there now," I told Harvey.

"Okay, Carol. Locate a site and get back with me."

"Harvey, I've found a location that is great for the Mesquite clinic," I told him later. "Right on the inside of the Interstate 635 loop, with great accessibility. The location is easy to find, even for out-of-towners. We'll cut our competition off at the pass; the women won't have to come all the way into Dallas for their abortion.

"You know," I continued, "I've dated a guy who does site selection for a fast-food restaurant, and he helped me pick the location. It's a free-standing building, right next door to the hospital. It'll be difficult for protesters to picket because of the private property lines. I don't think picketers can even get to the door. It's going to be a great location. We'll pile up some big numbers!"

"See what kind of lease you can work out for us, Carol."

I met with the owner of the building and negotiated our lease agreement. "I've worked out a turnkey lease with 100-percent finish-out, even down to the industrial-strength disposal—a double-action one that chops forward, reverses itself, and chops again as it reverses."

"That's great, Carol. When can we occupy the space?"

"September first."

We nickel-and-dimed the startup, with twelve thousand dollars taken out of the budget for the Mockingbird location and a ten thousand dollar loan from the bank. We bought used examination tables and re-covered an old couch. Harvey put his slippery sleight-of-hand routine to work again. He supplied stolen instruments and supplies from the hospital and from his private practice, just as he did when we built up the Mockingbird clinic.

We set up a separate corporation and named the facility "Women's Clinic of Mesquite." The officers were the same as in our other corporation, but we didn't issue stock.

Dr. Miller agreed to staff the Mesquite office, which meant we had a doctor on location all the time. We started out doing abortions six days a week in Mesquite and went to seven days in Dallas. Sunday was our best day from a profit-and-loss standpoint, because we were able to work a skeleton crew very effectively.

By the first month, the new clinic worked beautifully. We did over two hundred procedures in Mesquite and more than three hundred in North Dallas. I made more than twelve thousand five hundred dollars.

Our central telephone bank booked the appointments, then called the Mesquite clinic each afternoon to give their schedule. They called during the day to add other appointments, as necessary. If the Mesquite clinic had a procedure scheduled that was too big for Dr. Miller, they sent the patient to Dallas.

"Harvey, I'm very excited about the success of the new clinic," I exulted. "Our concept is right, I just know it." I congratulated myself on our success.

Harvey and I planned to operate five clinics and dominate the abortion business in the Dallas-Fort Worth metroplex. We'd use a single advertising budget for all five. We'd publish one local telephone number and one "800" number for out-of-town customers. All calls would be routed to the Mockingbird clinic, appointments booked, and the callers instructed as to which of our abortion clinics to use.

Harvey wanted a way to make money without all the stress of private obstetric practice—taking calls, delivering babies, late hours. He often commented, "Carol, you know, I don't like to get up in the middle of the night and deliver babies."

As for me, I wanted to make a million dollars a year. In order for both of us to have what we wanted, we needed to open five clinics, so we could do forty-thousand abortions annually.

With the second clinic open, our next goal was to hit the six-hundred-abortion-a-month mark by the end of the year. But if we were going to have the five clinics open and established by the end of 1984, we still had a lot of work to do.

As the business continued to grow, my ex-husband, Tom, reminded me again, "Carol Nan, you'd better get everything in writing."

"That's not necessary, Tom. If I can't trust Harvey, who can I trust?" After all, I was an officer in the corporation. My unwritten agreement with Harvey, as I understood it, was for a one-third interest in the clinics—as soon as he was ready to issue stock.

Increased Tensions

I felt very secure in my personal relationship with Harvey Johnson. There were no sexual ties, but I was very attached emotionally. I often pondered, *Harvey knows my every thought, and I think I know his. We love each other. I depend on Harvey, and he'll never hurt me. I'll never hurt him, either. We really are a family, as he says. We'll grow old together. It's the perfect relationship. He'll never leave me, because he doesn't have to—can't afford to. Ours is a business relationship, but with so many other benefits. We're friends, very close friends.*

Only one thing could potentially come between us, and that was Fredi. I was all for their arrangement while I worked with him. I knew instinctively that if I went to bed with Harvey, our relationship would be ruined. But Fredi couldn't be content with the emotional side of the coin. She wanted to run Harvey's business and be his sex partner, too. We were headed for some rough waters.

Most of the problems between Fredi and me were subtle—never discussed, but the tension was always there. I remember one time when Harvey asked me to come to his house and bring the office checkbook.

"Why are the last six checks written to you, Carol?" he demanded.

"I don't know. Let's look at what they were written for," I said, studying the check stubs. "That's reimbursement for lunch Friday and Saturday... Look, they're all reimbursements for lunches I paid for, lunches related to business. The particular places where we ate don't accept checks, so we used my cash."

Fredi seemed upset. It was obvious she had been going through the checkbook behind my back, trying to find something I'd done wrong.

The tension escalated when I started dating Ibrahim Oudeh, a Palestinian from Israel who graduated from medical school in Mexico and was now eligible for his residency.

Ibrahim and I met through Harvey and Fredi. Ibrahim had worked with Harvey, met Fredi, and the friendship between Ibrahim and Fredi deepened because Harvey was gone so much. The two of them enjoyed the same things, such as cooking and shopping. They spent a lot of free time together.

Fredi was quite attracted to Ibrahim. I knew it, and so did everyone else at the clinic. Harvey didn't seem to mind their friendship. Apparently, it took some pressure off him with Fredi. Harvey seemed quite confident that Ibrahim could not really compete with him for Fredi.

Then Ibrahim started spending more time at the clinic and began dating me. Kelly had just gone off to North Texas State University for her first semester while Joe Bob was back at the University of Texas. I was alone for the first time in my adult life.

I was open for a relationship with a man. I was lonely and wanted someone who would adjust to my schedule; Ibrahim fit the bill. He was available on demand and interesting when I chose to be with him. But our relationship made Fredi do a slow burn.

One evening right after Ibrahim and I started dating, Ibrahim came to me, quite upset. "One of Harvey's friends told him about a jewelry store going out of business. Harvey went to the sale and bought Fredi a wedding ring. I saw Fredi wearing it at his house last night."

Too stunned to talk, I just listened.

Finally the official announcement came—Harvey called me at the clinic.

"Fredi and I are getting married. We're going on a two-week trip for our honeymoon, so get the calendar and mark me out."

"When will you be gone?" I asked.

"Two weeks in February."

I marked out those weeks on the calendar, sat back in my chair, and cried. This news was sudden and devastating. I hurt so badly.

Then the jealousy inside me exploded. *I hate Fredi. She's sleeping with the man I love!* Deep in my heart, I finally admitted that I wanted Harvey.

I had to have revenge. Since Harvey and Fredi were planning a big honeymoon trip, Ibrahim and I needed to take a trip, too—in January, before their trip. "Ibrahim, let's go on a little vacation. Harvey and Fredi are taking off in February, and it's so hard on me when he's gone. I'd like to rest up before he leaves. Where would you like to go?"

"Mexico."

"Set it up, and I'll pay for it." I made sure everyone knew we were going on a trip in January—especially Fredi.

Fredi came into my office one day, saw Ibrahim standing next to me, turned and ran out of the clinic. *Maybe I'm having too much fun at Fredi's expense,* I mused.

Ibrahim followed her. They stood outside in the parking lot for over half an hour, with Ibrahim at times holding Fredi while she cried. Several employees reporting to work saw what was happening in the parking lot and came into my office and told me.

A new bitterness filled my relationship with Fredi. In my mind we were no longer just competing for Harvey, but for Ibrahim, too. Fredi's jealousy only fueled my fire and made me more competitive.

Whenever Fredi was around, I was careful to use terms of endearment with Ibrahim just to set her off. If Harvey were there, however, she couldn't do much more than steam.

"Ibrahim, Darling, would you hold this tray for me?" I beamed.

Fredi could barely contain herself as she sarcastically said, "'Ibrahim, darling'?"

Just before the marriage, I became very concerned about my status in the business. I took Harvey to lunch one day.

"Harvey, you have to protect me from Fredi," I said forthrightly, "in case something were to happen to you."

"I know," he agreed. "Give me some time to think about it, and I'll get back to you."

We talked again in a couple of weeks. "Carol, we'll purchase an insurance policy on my life for one-and-a-half-million dollars, which the clinic will pay for. You'll be the beneficiary, and in the event of my death you can use the money to buy the clinics from Fredi, free and clear."

I was relieved with the agreement. Cathy Byles, Wayne's wife, sold us the insurance policy, and I gave her the check for the first premium payment. I felt more secure now.

The wedding day finally arrived. Ibrahim, Kelly, and I went to the ceremony together. After the wedding we went to the reception, which soon became embarrassing. For the first time, I saw Harvey get drunk. He kissed me in front of everyone, and said, "I love you, Carol."

"I love you, too, Harvey." *But I'm not the one with the wedding ring.*

The whole scene was too much. We left early. I cried privately.

After they were married, Fredi wore her new title—Mrs. Harvey Johnson—with great zeal. She walked into the clinic and introduced herself to a new employee. "I'm Fredi Johnson, Dr. Johnson's wife."

When I overheard her introduction, I came unglued. "Don't come in here acting as if you're someone special because you are Mrs. Harvey Johnson!"

"I didn't," she smirked.

"You most certainly did!" I shot back. "You may be Dr. Johnson's wife, but that has no bearing on the bookkeeping job you do. Don't expect us to treat you differently. Your job hasn't changed."

She left.

My jealousy was out of control.

Fredi and I kept things in a constant turmoil at the clinic. Matters were so strained between us that we weren't concentrating properly on business expansion. I realized that my dream was in jeopardy; we had to resolve our differences. I tried to work it out with Fredi, but it was no use. We were firmly entrenched enemies.

Finally, as a last resort, I turned to Wayne Byles, Harvey's old friend and confidant. "Wayne, I know the Carol/Fredi problem is hindering the advancement of our business. We need some help."

"Carol, I'd like to bring in a business counselor I know," Wayne replied. "Maybe he'll be able to straighten things out."

"I'll talk to anyone who can get us back on the right track."

I was relieved, because I felt certain almost anyone we talked to would recommend that Fredi confine her activities with Harvey to the bedroom.

With help on the way from Wayne, Harvey and I settled down to plan for the future.

"Where do you think we should go next, Carol?" he asked.

"I think we should look closely at the Waco/Central Texas region. We're seeing a lot of women from that area, and there are no clinics in Central Texas that do late-term abortions."

"I'd like to go to the mid-cities area," Harvey responded. "We can do an end-run around Chuck by being on I-20 or I-30. We can really affect his Fort Worth clinic."

Things seemed to be moving in the right direction. Harvey began getting his business affairs in order to issue corporate stock. He had Cathy Byles talk to me about the best way to organize the business to accommodate my ownership. I believed Harvey was a man of his word. Also, I couldn't wait to tell Tom. I knew he'd be surprised that I'd actually pulled it off.

Within a short time, Wayne called. "I've made arrangements for you and Fredi to meet with the business counselor—a man named Jack Shaw. His office will call and set up a time."

Fredi and I each met with the counselor once. Jack Shaw was a strange man, like none other in my world. I couldn't figure him out, but I felt I had to understand him in order to be able to manipulate him. He didn't cooperate at all.

"Carol, why are you involved in the abortion business?" Jack asked, on one occasion.

"The bottom line is money. I can't make this kind of money anywhere else."

I kept waiting for Jack to tell me what he and Fredi were discussing, but he never would. That annoyed me.

After Fredi and I met with him separately, he asked for a joint meeting with Harvey, Wayne, Fredi, and me. We met at the corporate attorney's office, where he presented us with his initial findings. What I understood the counselor to say was, "Fredi, you should be happy; Harvey wants you to stay at home and be his wife."

I was jealous. I wanted that opportunity—to stay at home and be Harvey's wife—but I wasn't going to get it. I had to be satisfied with Fredi's departure from the clinic. I could certainly run the clinics more efficiently without her nose in my business, but I believed there would still be fireworks between us.

The counselor concluded, "I want to visit separately with Carol and Fredi four more times, and then have another meeting with the group."

Of course I agreed. I can talk to a guy anytime who is on my side—and Jack's suggestion to Fredi convinced me he was.

During my next meeting with the counselor, he said, "Carol, within thirty days something is going to happen."

"What do you mean?"

"I'm not sure. But within thirty days, someone will be leaving the clinic," he repeated, enigmatically.

I left his office with those words ringing in my ears. He had to be referring to Fredi!

11

....

LIGHTS, CAMERA, ACTION

ONE DAY HARVEY called and informed me about a phone call from an ex-employee. "Carol, Dana called and Channel 4 has been sending reporters into clinics to see if they'll do abortions on women who aren't pregnant."

"Uh-oh... We've had a rash of negative pregnancy tests recently," I remarked.

"How many?"

"I'll have to look. How does Dana know?"

"Her husband has coffee regularly with someone who works for Channel 4. That's how she knows." He paused. "Where do you keep the negative pregnancy test reports?"

"In a separate file, up front."

"Go up there and count how many have been in recently."

I went to the front and counted six negative pregnancy tests from the past couple of weeks.

"Did we tell them they were pregnant?" Harvey asked, when I relayed the information.

"Ibrahim did sonograms."

"Yeah, and Ibrahim finds almost everyone to be pregnant," Harvey said, a grimace in his voice. "Can you stay late at the clinic tonight? Fredi and I will come down. Ask Jan and Ibrahim to stay, too. We'll go through the negative pregnancy tests to see what's going on."

"I'll be here, Harvey."

We've Been Set Up!

When I hung up the telephone, my mind raced back a few days. Janet, one of the laboratory technicians, had come to me and reported, "Carol, we just had another negative pregnancy test, the sixth in the last few days. Something is going on."

"Where is the patient?"

133

"Dr. Oudeh is doing a sonogram."

I joined Ibrahim in the sonogram room. "How does it look?"

"She's pregnant," he replied. "See there?" He pointed to a shadow on the sonogram screen. Ibrahim patted the girl and said, "Baby, you're pregnant, but it's very early. That's why the pregnancy test you took showed negative. Please get dressed and come to the office so we can talk."

I left the room knowing that Ibrahim would do everything he could to get that woman to have the procedure that day.

Harvey had approached me back in December and asked, "What do you think about sending Ibrahim to sonogram school in Houston?"

"That'd be great, Harvey. We need a sonogram technician. Have you talked to him?"

"No, but I will. Do you think he'll do it?" he asked.

"I know he needs some income." I thought a minute, then said, "I'm sure he will. He needs to do something while he's applying to residency programs."

Ibrahim happily agreed, attended the school, and returned, eager to do sonograms and make money. His function was to perform a routine sonogram on any patient over twelve weeks into her pregnancy, as well as on women whose pregnancy tests were negative (to see if we could prove any of them were actually pregnant). Ibrahim made fifty dollars per sonogram, and some of the doctors individually paid him extra to assist them in doing abortions.

Sometimes the sonogram cast enough doubt on the pregnancy test that we were able to sell another abortion. It was a good technique.

"After all, it costs as much to get in a non-pregnant one as a pregnant one," Harvey reasoned.

About six o'clock in the evening, Harvey and Fredi arrived to review the negative pregnancy tests. Ibrahim was already there. That night, I saw a new side of Harvey Johnson—the angry, vindictive, paranoid side. He was scared.

We had dinner across the street at a local restaurant, then returned to the clinic to do our research.

I went to the drop file and pulled out the records. "Here they are. Some of them didn't even fill out forms. They were probably walk-in pregnancy tests that came in during procedure hours, and no one had time to spend with them."

"Here's one that filled out the forms," Harvey said, pulling a file from the stack. "Pull the schedule for Wednesday. Was a patient named Linda Wells scheduled for a procedure?"

"Linda Wells, six weeks pregnant, scheduled at 8:30 A.M. We have an address and everything."

"What's the name of the reporter Dana said is doing the report?" Harvey asked.

"Laura Randle."

"Get the telephone directory and look up Laura Randle."

"Here it is…The address is 1416 Meadow Lane, telephone 555-196-0579."

"That's the same address listed on this chart!" Harvey exclaimed. "She only changed her name. Laura Randle was in our clinic, we did a pregnancy test on her that was negative, and then we did a sonogram… What do you remember about her, Ibrahim?"

"Let me see the chart… Just from looking at the chart, I don't remember anything. My normal routine is to do a sonogram and then tell her if she's pregnant or not."

"Do you remember if you told Laura Randle she was pregnant?"

"No. I don't remember anything specific about her."

I suspected that Ibrahim found every woman "pregnant," and that he tried to convince them all to have an abortion. I just knew we were caught, red-handed. We'd been doing abortions on women who weren't pregnant, and I hadn't been willing to admit it or put a stop to it. I'd turned my eyes the other way. *After all, I'm not the doctor. The doctor is responsible for the medical procedures.*

But what abortionist, working on a straight commission, is going to tell a woman who has signed her consent form and has already paid in full that she isn't pregnant? I closed my eyes to the sonograms and collected my twenty-five dollars.

Later, in recalling this event, I would remember that Laura Randle had been in our clinic as a gynecology patient several months before she did the report. Harvey and I personally gave her special attention because she was with Channel 4. It's hard to imagine now that we were so rattled the night we reviewed the files that we didn't piece it together sooner. Laura Randle had been setting us up for months, and we never realized it.

I rejoined the conversation. "Harvey, what do we do now?"

"Let me think about it. I need to talk to our attorney, because I really don't know *what* to do...wait until we're contacted, I guess. I think they'll contact us before they air the story," he theorized.

He turned to me then. "Be very careful when a pregnancy test turns up negative. Tell Janet you want to see every one of them as soon as you get negative results. Question each one carefully and tell them the pregnancy test we use is not the most sensitive diagnostic device, that they still could be pregnant. Tell them we'd like them to wait two weeks and come back for another pregnancy test at that time. We can beat Laura Randle at this game!"

Laura Randle has already beaten us, I thought.

It turned out Laura Randle herself had never come into the clinic for a pregnancy test. She sent in three different women over several days.

The first girl came in with a urine sample she knew to be negative before entering the clinic. The lab did a pregnancy test and Janet told her, "Your urine test shows to be negative, but you could still be pregnant. The test we ran is not sensitive enough to pick up an early pregnancy. Would you like us to do a sonogram and an examination, so you'll know and not have to worry?"

"Yes, I would," the girl agreed.

Ibrahim did the sonogram, and when he finished, he said, "Yeah, babe, you're pregnant. Do you have your money? Want to do it today?"

"Not today," she responded.

We found out later that after the girl left the clinic, she was once again tested by a doctor hired by the television station to be sure she wasn't pregnant.

In our research that evening we must have discovered the first girl Channel 4 sent in. By the time the second and third girls came in, we had our new system in place. They were each told a different story; we weren't about to get trapped again.

Why Now?

Channel 4's investigation of our clinic could not have happened at a busier time. Wayne and Cathy Byles were busily installing a new book-keeping system. Harvey was getting his business affairs in order so we could finally issue the clinic stock. Fredi and I were in the process of trying to make peace with each other, with the counselor's help.

Dana's call about Laura Randle came right after my second visit with the counselor, when he told me that within thirty days someone would leave the clinic. I was looking forward to Fredi's imminent departure.

Business was booming. Our advertising covered a five-state area, and each month our practice continued to grow. In my mind, we were about to really take off. Soon we would be ready to open our third, fourth, and fifth clinics. I would finally be a millionaire! I could hardly wait.

I had been promising each of the kids a new car. While they were home from school for the summer, we looked around.

"What kind of car do you want, Joe Bob?"

"A new pickup."

But my dream was for him to have a new sports car.

"What kind of car do you want, Kelly?"

"A Mazda."

I wanted them to have identical sports cars—just alike, except for the color. Kelly's would be pink and Joe Bob's brown.

"Well, I want a black one if I'm going to get a sports car," Joe Bob insisted.

I had to compromise with him, but Kelly always tried to please me. On July 2, I bought two brand new Datsun 280 ZX's—one pink and one black.

Some real estate dealings I had with Ibrahim were beginning to go sour and consume what little spare time I had. We had previously bought some rental property together (mostly to aggravate Fredi), and the real estate market in Texas was beginning a long downward slide. The previous April, Ibrahim had come to me, proposing the final deal we would do together. "My family are all butchers in Israel," he told me. "I'd like to buy a butcher shop in Richardson. We can make about eight thousand dollars a month—clear profit."

That stirred up old memories of Daddy—when he worked in the butcher shop during my early childhood.

"How will we run a butcher shop?"

"I have a friend who's a butcher," Ibrahim countered. "He'll run it for a one-third interest in the business."

I co-signed a note at the bank for fifty thousand dollars, and on May 2 we became the proud owners of Promenade Meat Center in

Richardson, Texas. One month after it opened, the butcher shop owed twelve thousand dollars to suppliers, and I had already fed it two thousand five hundred dollars. I had to fire Randy, our one-third owner. With two employees, I began a self-designed crash course in the butcher business. Somehow, I managed to keep Harvey from knowing about any of it.

While I was preoccupied with this dubious business interest, Harvey was consumed with fear about Laura Randle and her investigation. He was crazy with worry because we hadn't yet heard from her. I had never seen him act so strangely. "Harvey, why are you so worried?" I asked.

"This could ruin the clinic, and we're just beginning to make headway."

Secretly, I believed Harvey was afraid Sheryl Mason's death would come to light, along with all the other messed-up abortions he'd concealed. His medical reputation would be ruined if that happened. I realized it was a possibility, but I had come to consider fear as our greatest enemy, not discovery.

I had an uncanny intuition that everything would be all right, and tried to reassure him. "Harvey, we just have to let this crisis pass and then move on. Everything is going to be fine." But my attempted reassurances only seemed to convince him I was crazy.

It wasn't long before Laura Randle called the clinic. "Is Dr. Johnson in? This is Laura Randle with Channel 4 News."

The call was transferred to me. "May I help you?"

"This is Laura Randle with Channel 4 News. May I speak with Dr. Johnson?"

"He's not in at the moment. May I take a message?"

"Yes. Ask him to call me at the station." And she gave me the phone number. "When do you think he'll call?" she persisted.

"I'm not certain, but I would imagine he'd call this afternoon," I hedged.

"Thank you."

I quickly called Harvey's private practice office. "Harvey, Laura Randle just called for you. She wants you to call her back."

"What did she say?"

"Nothing. She wanted to talk to you."

"I don't want to call her, but I have to...don't I?"

"Yes, you do. We really don't have anything to worry about. I've seen this happen to other clinics, and it only helped their business."

What seemed like an eternity passed before Harvey called me back. "She wants to interview me on-camera."

"Did she say what the interview was about?"

"No, she was elusive, but wants the interview. I can't do it. It can't come out that I am the medical director for an abortion clinic."

Fine time to figure that out, I thought.

"Carol, you'll have to do the interview."

When the going gets rough...just throw Carol to the lions! "I don't think she will interview me. She wants the medical director."

"I'm going to talk to the attorney, but I think you're the one who ought to do the interview. We'll talk later tonight," he promised.

I was aware of how those interviews went from my experience with Chuck. Anything I said would be twisted and used against me. I reasoned, *I don't want to do that interview. I want no part of it. But how can I tell Harvey 'No'?*

Harvey called that evening at his regular time. "Carol, you've got to do the interview with Laura Randle next week. You know I can't do it."

"I know, Harvey."

"You'll do just fine," he assured me. "I'll see you at the clinic tomorrow. Good night, Carol. I love you."

"I love you, too, Harvey." Amazing what we'll say when we're in a pinch.

On Saturday night, I was cleaning up the back area at the clinic, angry that Harvey, Fredi, and Ibrahim were up front, talking. I hit the cabinet with one of the hoses from the suction machine, and it bounced off and caught me in the eye. It cut my eyelid, and I just knew my eye was going to be black. Crying and bleeding, I rushed into Harvey's office, where Fredi, Ibrahim, and Harvey were.

"I cut my eye," I sobbed. "I can't do the interview."

Harvey was crushed, but sensed he had pushed me too far. He consoled me. "Everything is going to be all right, Carol." It was the first time in a long time he had given me consolation.

That solved the problem. I didn't have to do the interview.

Fredi came in my office early the next week and said, "You don't have a black eye."

"It's one of the marvels of makeup, Fredi," I replied sarcastically.

She thought she'd caught me in a lie, and she actually had. I didn't have a black eye, but I wasn't going to hang myself to cover for Harvey again.

We sent a letter instead of doing the interview. I signed the letter, realizing I was setting myself up again.

On Wednesday afternoon, Harvey, Jan Batson (his former nurse), and I were in my office when an employee burst in. "A patient just came in and said there is someone outside the clinic filming something for the news!"

Harvey's face contorted. I stood up. "Don't leave, Carol!" he screamed as he reached for me.

"Harvey, I was only going to lower the thermostat." I turned to the employee. "Thanks for telling us." I closed the door.

I could see the fear sweeping over Harvey in waves. He turned to me. "Don't move. Stay right there. Jan, you go out the back door, come up between the buildings, and see what's happening."

"Okay." Jan walked out.

Harvey's face was red, full of anger…which was directed at me! He had never before talked to me in that manner. I was scared of Harvey for the first time in my life. I had seen him angry with Fredi, and Alma Jean, his housekeeper, had told me about his violent rages—but this was a first for me.

More than the cameras, I was concerned with what was happening in my office. For the first time in our relationship, I feared Harvey might strike me. I had experienced that as a little child, and knew what to do— be very quiet. I didn't say a word. I was completely still.

A relationship of years was being destroyed before my eyes, exploding like a nuclear bomb, incinerating our friendship in such a way that it could never be rebuilt. I now saw that Harvey habitually abused me, abused Fredi, abused everyone. I had never before seen that.

I would never intentionally hurt Harvey, but I now realized he would hurt me if it served his purpose. Our relationship didn't matter as much to him as his career and reputation.

"Harvey, I need to go to the front to see what's going on in the office," I delicately suggested.

"Sure, sure." He dismissed me.

The front office was buzzing, everyone looking out the window to see what was going on. I spoke in a reassuring tone of voice. "Don't be concerned. If they're filming us, we don't want to be filmed staring at them. Let's get back to work."

Nervous laughter followed, and we started back to work.

Jan came in through the front door. "They're gone. They were filming what looked like a news segment. They were zeroing in on the clinic while the reporter talked."

Harvey uttered an expletive, something he never did.

What was going on with this man? We had killed a woman and maimed several others, yet I had never seen Harvey Johnson as upset as he was now. He was angry at me, almost as if he blamed me for the whole thing. I didn't understand.

"They'll investigate the clinic," he said, morosely.

"Who will?"

"The National Abortion Federation."

"I don't think they've ever investigated any abortion clinic," I replied. "When The Women's Center had a death at their clinic a few years ago, cameras from Channel 8 burst into their staff meeting and the story aired right after the death. It helped their business, remember? No one investigated them. No one is going to investigate us over a news report. Don't be so paranoid."

Who'll Be the Scapegoat?

I started to dread Harvey's presence. I dreaded the days he worked in the clinic, but I had no choice; I had to be there. He needed me, especially now.

The week before the expose aired for the first time, Harvey made a request. "Carol, I know you want to go to your twenty-five-year class reunion this weekend, but with all this going on, I wish you wouldn't."

"I won't go if you don't want me to, Harvey. I'll stay here."

"I'd just feel better if you did."

Another sacrifice made for Harvey.

Everything was crumbling around me, but I was calm. I couldn't understand the inner peace I felt. I missed my next appointment with Jack Shaw, the counselor, but didn't even call to cancel.

A new chasm developed between Harvey and me. I didn't understand his irrational fear. I tried to reassure him, but he didn't understand why I was so calm. He kept telling me how upset he was. I kept reassuring him, "Everything is going to be all right. Harvey, any publicity—bad or good—helps business. They'll all know where to find us, at least."

Harvey had lost his sense of humor and was starting to lose weight. "This Laura Randle diet has taken ten pounds off me already," he said in a feeble attempt at levity.

During the weekend, Channel 4 started to air an hourly teaser; they would have a revelation about Dallas abortion clinics on the 10 P.M. news the following Wednesday. We knew which clinic it would be.

On Monday, in the middle of the night, my father called. "Carol, your Grandmother Taylor just passed away. We'll call you about the funeral arrangements in the morning."

I was very sad when I hung up the telephone. One of my goals was to buy my grandmother a new car—she had been driving an old wreck for years.

Tuesday morning at 8 A.M., I had breakfast with Cathy Byles in order to discuss my compensation as a stockholder. She explained how my checks would be written. I finished the meeting and rushed to work.

Later in the day, Mother called about the funeral arrangements. "Carol Nan, the funeral is going to be Wednesday afternoon."

"Mother, can you postpone the funeral to Thursday? I need to be at the clinic tomorrow. We'll work tomorrow and be in San Saba tomorrow night." Even as I asked, I realized it was a major favor to ask of my mother, but I couldn't have Harvey going berserk while I was at my grandmother's funeral.

Mother was upset, but agreed to postpone the funeral. With the news story breaking Wednesday night at 10 and Harvey scheduled to work at the clinic, I just couldn't leave. Harvey needed me more than ever before.

Wednesday was tense, with Harvey in the clinic and my mind diverted by the preparations for my grandmother's funeral. Somehow, we got through it. I was relieved to go to San Saba with Kelly. Joe Bob and his girlfriend drove down in his car. For a short period of time I could escape the unbearable pressure.

We arrived at my parents' home in time for the 10 P.M. news. It was terrible. The expose showed the reporter walking into our clinic, as well as a shot of Ibrahim and me walking across the parking lot into the clinic. They aired sketches of how we sold abortions to women who weren't pregnant, and in the background they played Ibrahim's voice, which the reporter had recorded with a hidden microphone, saying, "Yeah, babe, you're pregnant. Do you have your money? Want to do it today?"

My stomach turned. I was physically ill. I called Harvey. He was quiet, dejected. He could hardly talk.

"It was terrible, Carol."

"It'll be all right, Harvey. You'll see."

"No, it won't. How soon can you get back to Dallas?"

"I'll be at your home tomorrow night in time to watch the next segment."

"See you then."

I called Ibrahim. "Did you see it?"

"Yes. Harvey's going to blame me for everything."

"No. Harvey wouldn't do something like that. He'll be loyal. He'll defend you, Ibrahim."

"No. Just watch, Carol. It'll be all my fault."

"I don't think so. We'll talk about it tomorrow. See you then."

Ibrahim joined me Thursday morning for the funeral. "Carol, I'm going to take the blame for this. I just know it."

"Harvey wouldn't do that to you. You were following directions. He'll protect you. Just watch," I promised, believing it would be true.

The funeral seemed endless. I went on internal cruise control. I still had this strange peace inside me despite the turmoil surrounding me. I felt as if I needed to let the dust settle down, and then Harvey would be himself again.

Suddenly, a new thought popped into my mind. *Maybe I'm going to be the scapegoat, not Ibrahim.* I pushed that idea aside quickly. *It'll be all right. Harvey won't do that to me.*

Finally, we were on our way back to Dallas. We didn't arrive in time to go to Harvey's before the news, so we went straight to my house and watched the broadcast.

Afterward, I called Harvey. "Sorry, Harvey. We were late. I just got back in town and stopped at home to watch the news. I'm on my way to your house."

"Don't come over, Carol. The attorneys are here. I'll talk to you later." Harvey's voice was different, offhand. Something was really wrong.

"Harvey, are you all right?"

"Yes, I'm fine. Wayne wants to meet you for breakfast with Billie,"
—the director of our Women's Clinic of Mesquite—"at the Executive
Inn. Can you be there at eight o'clock?"

"I can be there."

During breakfast, Wayne kept asking me, "Carol, why are you out
of control?" I didn't feel out of control, but it was as if he wanted me,
willed for me, to lose control. I could hardly keep from laughing at the
manipulative game I knew he was playing. But why was he doing it?

We repeatedly went over my daily activities. I finally concluded
that Wayne was going to have Billie take my place temporarily, to take
some of the pressure off me. He seemed to be nervous about what my
reaction to that news would be.

When I got to the clinic, I received roses from the staff and a bouquet from Billie. The employees rallied behind me and supported me
with many hugs and much love, trying to comfort me in the aftermath
of the negative expose.

But Harvey didn't call at his regular times, which was very strange.
I tried to call him, but each time his response was, "Carol, I can't talk
now."

At the end of the day, Harvey told Ibrahim not to come back to
the clinic. I was really surprised. Ibrahim had been right, and I was
wrong. Harvey didn't stand by him!

I drove home Friday evening, thinking that Ibrahim was right,
after all. I remembered thinking earlier, *Maybe I'm going to be the scapegoat for what happened at the clinic.* Then, I reasoned, *I'm the most likely
candidate to be sacrificed next. Harvey's actions for the last few days make
sense. I'm going to be blamed. Harvey is going to use me after all. We aren't
family—and never were.*

*Harvey is the one who hired Ibrahim. He's the medical director, not
me. But I'm going to be blamed for the things he trained Ibrahim to do.
They're going to use my personal relationship with Ibrahim to try to prove
we were working together—that his false diagnoses were my fault.*

I also remembered Tom admonishing me to get everything down
on paper. "Cover yourself, Carol Nan. You're wide open."

"Tom, this man will not hurt me. I trust him."

That conversation rang in my ears. How naive could I be?

I went to dinner that night with Kelly, Joe Bob, and their dates.

Not much was said about the news. I went to bed early, because Saturday was always a big day. If I had only known how big!

Dressed in my scrub suit, I arrived early, as usual, and went to work. Harvey came in at nine o'clock, depressed, dejected, withdrawn.

Wayne and Harvey met together most of the day. Jack Shaw, the counselor, joined them at about mid-morning. I went through the motions of working, but my inquisitive mind was working overtime. Why was Jack meeting with Wayne and Harvey? I already knew I was going to be replaced temporarily, but what else were they discussing? I believed they were discussing me. I wanted very much to be a fly on the wall in that meeting.

At about noon, a telephone call came from a young woman who had been in for an abortion at six weeks into her term, but did not come back for her two-week checkup. "I can feel a foot in my vagina," she said.

I looked at her chart and found her abortion had been done some fourteen weeks earlier. If her fetus had been missed, she was now at least twenty weeks into her pregnancy. Dr. Leggett was her doctor, and he did occasionally miss one. I told the receptionist to ask her to come in immediately.

Personal terror. The only big-baby abortionist who could do one free—because we had missed the baby—was Harvey. But I had sworn he would never do another big-baby abortion. What could I do?

Later in the day, the young woman came in for her examination. Harvey checked her. Afterward, Harvey, Billie, and I discussed the situation.

"Leggett missed it. She's right—the baby's foot is dangling in her vagina."

"Harvey, it's twenty weeks along! That baby has been growing for fourteen more weeks."

"I know."

Harvey was in no shape to do a "big" abortion. To make matters worse, he didn't want to put the girl to sleep because of the extra cost.

I looked at Billie and said, "Let me out of here before you start this one." I could just see him blowing the abortion and pulling a bowel through the vagina again.

"Okay, Carol."

Wayne met me in the hall. "Carol, can you join Jack and me in Harvey's office?" I went inside.

When I was seated, Wayne began. "Carol, it might be better if you kept a low profile for a while. Perhaps you can go to Oklahoma and set up an operation there."

"What do you mean, Wayne?"

"With all the negative publicity lately, you need to stay out of this clinic. You'll be taken care of. We just need to find somewhere else for you to go right now. You don't need to come in tomorrow. Billie will handle everything."

I was relieved to hear Wayne say I would be taken care of. They only wanted me to go to Oklahoma.

What I later found out is that Wayne and Jack had earlier become deeply involved in a conversation about abortion—and about me. Wayne told Jack he was pleased I was *getting out* of the business, and that he would completely sever ties with it himself it weren't for his commitment to remaining behind to accomplish another goal: to lead his lifelong friend, Harvey Johnson, out of the abortion industry. But why? Why did Wayne want Harvey—or *me*, for that matter—to leave such a lucrative occupation?

I left Harvey's office and went to the back to gather my things. As I passed by the room where Harvey and Billie were preparing to redo the missed abortion, something unusual happened: For the first time, the smell of death in the back part of the clinic nauseated me.

But at the same time, a part of me wanted to go in that room and help Harvey, comfort him.

Billie saw me and came out to talk. "They want me to do your job, but your friendship is more important to me than this job. I won't do it if you don't want me to."

I looked her in the eyes and knew it wouldn't matter how I responded to her. I said, "Do the job, Billie. I'll feel better, knowing you're taking care of it." *After all, it's only temporary.*

I went to my office, wrote myself a check, and met Jack in the hallway. Together we walked out of the clinic.

"What's going to happen next, Jack?"

"I'm not sure, Carol, but everything will work out for the best."

I walked out of the clinic with Jack Shaw, the strange counselor I had known for only twenty-five days. As we walked away from the clinic, I remember thinking, *I hope I can trust Jack. I haven't been a very good judge of character up to now—yet there is something different about him. Besides, I have no one else to turn to. I have to trust him.* It was as though an enormous weight was being lifted off my shoulders.

I felt peaceful.

12

·························

THE DIFFERENCE
AFTER ONE PRAYER

KELLY, I'M GOING to church in the morning. Will you go with me?" The silence at the dinner table was arresting.

"Church? Yes, Mom…I'll go with you." Kelly's assent was just what I needed to hear.

The next morning, Kelly and I went to a little church that was meeting in a portable building in Plano. This was the place where Jack Shaw, my counselor, ministered. I entered the church carrying the weight of 35,001 abortions, a mother's death, and multiple botched abortions. Yes, 35,001 abortions—the babies of 35,000 other mothers and my own baby. Six years of involvement in the abortion industry had cost a lot. The price was much higher than I ever imagined.

I left church believing the sermon had been prepared just for me.

Kelly and I picked up Joe Bob and his girlfriend for lunch. It was wonderful, just spending time with my family and not running off to work.

After lunch, I found myself alone and took the opportunity to review the events of the past twenty-five days, especially the meetings with Jack. In our first meeting, with Wayne, Harvey, and Fredi, he seemed to be on my side. The second time I met with him, I wasn't so sure. That time, he seemed to be able to see inside me…I knew I had to turn the tables on him and get control of the interview.

I started asking him questions. "Are you a preacher?" To this day, I don't know why I asked him that.

"Yes, I am, Carol."

"Well, I want you to know that I'm a Christian, too. I pray every day. I keep a Bible in the right-hand drawer of my desk, and I tithe on all the money I make."

"That's good, Carol—but those things don't make you a Christian."

My Fateful Meeting with Jack—and God

It surprised me that he wasn't impressed with my tithing. I regrouped quickly and asked, "What in the world are you doing in this situation?"

"God sent me."

This man was crazy! I shot back, "I believe God has put me in the clinics, too—to help women. We counsel every woman who comes into our clinic."

When I stopped telling him about how good I was, he said, "I've been praying with some other folks about this, and I believe God has given me thirty days to get my job done. Something is going to happen within thirty days. Someone is going to be leaving the clinic."

"What do you mean, 'something is going to happen'?"

"I'm not sure, Carol."

Someone will be leaving the clinic all right, but it won't be me. It'll be Fredi. I changed the topic. "Jack, how did you and Wayne get acquainted? I'm really curious as to why Wayne chose you to be the counselor to help us with our problem."

"It's a long story, but I'll make it as brief as I can. About five years ago, a man I'd counseled worked with Wayne and set up an appointment for us to visit with him. We went to see Wayne at his office in Garland. I shared Christ with him, and it made him quite upset at the time. I hadn't heard from Wayne again until just recently, when he related his story to me.

"Wayne told me he had been driving down North Central Expressway in all the heavy traffic—and with a very heavy heart. He began to turn to God for help. At that time, he began to remember everything I had shared with him five years earlier in his office. It all came back to him so clearly while on that expressway. He prayed to receive Jesus Christ as his Lord and Savior, right then. He wanted me to be the first to know.

"I told him it was wonderful and how thrilled I was for him. I encouraged him to visit with me soon." And then Jack's eyes bored into me.

"Carol, since that time, Wayne and I have met together on several occasions, and I've helped him in some other areas. He's very interested in helping you, Harvey, and Fredi make peace with God, as he has done. God and Wayne are the reasons I'm here today with you.

"I know Wayne has tried to share his faith with you in his own way, but he doesn't believe he's able to say what needs to be said to help you. Isn't it true that Wayne has spoken to you?"

"Yes, I guess he has." It was all well and good that Wayne wanted to help us. With the one-track mind I had at the time, I thought I could endure whatever Wayne had up his sleeve—if it would get Fredi out of the clinic. Jack kept talking.

"Carol, everyone is searching for attention, recognition, security, acceptance, and identity... Call it what you will, everyone is really searching for the same thing—love. And we search for it in all the wrong places. The greatest need we have in life is to be loved. It's as if we go around, screaming inside, 'For God's sake, won't someone pay attention to me, recognize me, accept me, love me?'

"Although we long for love that's genuine, most of the love we find is counterfeit. Every outreach we make, every person we turn to, fails us—or we fail them. We walk away from relationship after relationship, beat up and hurt. We carry a lot of pain inside, pain caused by damaged relationships."

Jack's words were hitting a tender spot inside me, and hitting it hard! But I couldn't pull myself away—and was surprised to realize I didn't really want to.

"You see, Carol, most of our relationships are based on performance. We think we're loved when people do to us and for us what we think or feel should be done to us and for us. Do you know what I mean?"

"Yes, I'm afraid I do." Did I ever!

"Carol, the moment we were born we started reaching out to our family, to our parents, to love us. If they're following God's plan, we receive genuine love, but if they're doing the best they know how—apart from God—their love is counterfeit.

"We reach out to family, friends, the opposite sex, material possessions, education, sports, accomplishments, social status, work, professions, and other sources to give us the recognition and attention we crave. Can you identify with what I'm saying?"

"Yes." Something was beginning to disturb me at the very center of my soul.

"Carol, in our first meeting, you said you're in this job because of money. Am I correct?"

"Yes, I did say that."

"I'd like for you to read this passage," he said, handing me his Bible.

> He is conceited and understands nothing. He has an unhealthy interest in controversies and arguments that result in envy, quarreling, malicious talk, evil suspicions and protracted wrangling and wearing discussion and perpetual friction among men who are corrupted in mind and bereft of the truth, who imagine that godliness or righteousness is a source of profit—a money-making business, a means of livelihood. From such withdraw.

> And it is, indeed, a source of immense profit, for godliness accompanied with contentment—that contentment which is a sense of inward sufficiency—is great and abundant gain.

> For we brought nothing into the world, and obviously we cannot take anything out of the world;

> But if we have food and clothing, with these we shall be content (satisfied).

> But those who crave to be rich fall into temptation and a snare, and into many foolish (useless, godless) and hurtful desires that plunge men into ruin and destruction and miserable perishing.

> For the love of money is a root of all evils; it is through this craving that some have been led astray, and have wandered from the faith and pierced themselves through with many acute [mental] pangs.

> But as for you, O man of God, flee from all these things; aim at and pursue righteousness—that is, right standing with God and true goodness; godliness (which is the loving fear of God and Christ-likeness), faith, love, steadfastness (patience) and gentle-heartedness.

> Fight the good fight of the faith; lay hold of the eternal life to which you were summoned, and confess the good confession [of faith] before many witnesses.

> In the presence of God Who preserves alive all living things, and of Christ Jesus Who in His testimony before Pontius Pilate made the good confession, I [solemnly]

> charge you to keep all His precepts unsullied and flaw-
> less, irreproachable until the appearing of our Lord Jesus
> Christ, the Anointed One.
>
> Which will be shown forth in His own proper time
> by the blessed, only Sovereign, the King of kings and the
> Lord of lords. (1 Timothy 6:4-15)

"Carol, is it possible you're in this business because of the love of money—greed?" he said when I finished reading.

"Yes, I suppose it is." *I'm really in trouble now. Everything in me is going crazy. He's hitting me right where I live!*

"Guess what, Carol?" he continued. "Money won't satisfy you. It too will be used to destroy relationships, because you can't buy people. You can use money to try to buy love, but true love can't be bought. Counterfeit love can be. Do you think you've ever tried to buy love?"

"Yes, of course I have." *What's with this guy, anyway?* I thought, trying to rebel against this whole uncomfortable process. *I'm not here to work on me—I'm here to work on Fredi!*

"You see, Carol," he went on, "even when we use money to express our love, it has a string attached to it—most of the time. We want something in return. When we get it, we feel loved; when we don't get what we want, we feel unloved.

"Carol, the Bible says, 'God is love.' He alone is the source of authentic love. God is the only one who can love unconditionally. When we try to love God's way—just because we know we're supposed to—we fail. The Bible says, 'Love your enemies; do good to those who would despitefully use you.' Carol, God requires you to love Fredi. Have you tried?"

Where in the world was this conversation going? "Yes, but it hasn't worked."

"Thank God it hasn't, Carol."

"Why do you say that?" I was totally confused now.

"Because your inability to solve the problem with Fredi has brought you to the place where you can make the greatest discovery of your life."

"What do you mean?"

"You can discover the love you have been searching for all your life, and begin to love Fredi as God wants you to. And not just Fredi, but anyone else you may have a problem loving. Do you know why you fight with Fredi and can't love her?"

"No, I guess not."

"Let's look at another passage." Again, he handed me his Bible.

> What leads to strife (discord and feuds) and how do
> conflicts (quarrels and fightings) originate among you?
> Do they not arise from your sensual desires that are ever
> warring in your bodily members?
>
> You are jealous and covet [what others have] and
> your desires go unfulfilled; [so] you become murderers.
> [To hate is to murder as far as your hearts are concerned.]
> You burn with envy and anger and are not able to obtain
> [the gratification, the contentment and the happiness
> that you seek], so you fight and war. (James 4:1-2)

When I finished reading, he asked, "Carol, are you jealous of Fredi?"

"Yes, I am." There, I admitted it!

"God wants you to love her and to be happy for her. He wants you to care for her just as He does."

That sounds good, but this guy doesn't know Fredi, or the people I've been dealing with all my life. He lives in a fantasy world. Besides, isn't he just telling Fredi the same things? My suspicious mind began to whirl with excuses.

"You see, Carol," Jack said patiently, "if God is the only one who can love unconditionally, then God has to be inside *us* loving as only He can—*through* us."

I can sure give him a list of folks God would have trouble loving. "How does that happen?" I asked.

"The Bible says, 'God's love is shed abroad in our hearts by the Holy Spirit who is given unto us.' Let's read 1 John 4:7-15." Here came that Bible again.

> Beloved, let us love one another; for love is [springs]
> from God; and he who loves [his fellowmen] is begotten
> (born) of God and is coming [progressively] to know and
> understand God [to perceive and recognize and get a
> better and clearer knowledge of Him].
>
> He who does not love has not become acquainted

with God [does not and never did know Him] for God is love.

In this the love of God was made manifest (displayed), where we are concerned: in that God sent His Son, the only begotten or unique [Son], into the world so we might live through Him.

In this is love: not that we loved God, but that He loved us and sent His Son to be the propitiation (the atoning sacrifice) for our sins.

Beloved, if God loved us so [very much], we also ought to love one another.

No man has at any time [yet] seen God. But if we love one another, God abides (lives and remains) in us and His love [that love which is essentially His] is brought to completion (to its full maturity, runs its full course, is perfected) in us!

By this we come to know (perceive, recognize and understand) that we abide (live and remain) in Him and He in us: because He has given (imparted) to us of His [Holy] Spirit.

And [besides] we ourselves have seen (have deliberately and steadfastly contemplated) and bear witness that the Father has sent the Son [as the] Savior of the world.

Anyone who confesses (acknowledges, owns) that Jesus is the Son of God, God abides (lives, makes His home) in him, and he (abides, lives, makes his home) in God.

"Carol, the word *confess* includes acknowledging Jesus Christ as Lord over our lives. For Him to be the Lord of our lives means He begins to reign in our hearts, ruling our lives in every way, loving—as only He can—through us; even loving the 'Fredi's' in our lives."

He's certainly beginning to make sense, but I didn't come to the counselor to be preached to. I came to make peace with Fredi. But—could he be right?

Jack wasn't finished yet. "Now, if Christ Jesus isn't living as Lord of our lives, then we're trying to be in control ourselves, missing the mark God intends for us to hit, living where we shouldn't be living, doing what is displeasing to God. We're loving the best we know how, but it's not good enough. We're living in sin as far as God is concerned. In confession, we acknowledge we've been trying to run our own lives.

"Carol, would you like to make peace with Fredi and begin to love her God's way?"

My hands were twisting in my lap. "You're asking a lot."

"No, I'm not. God is."

Great. Now he's got God right in the middle—between Fredi and me. If I'm going to please God, I'm going to have to love Fredi and want what's best for her instead of what's best for me. No way!

"Carol," Jack concluded, "I wouldn't be much of a salesman if I didn't offer to close the deal. Would you like me to pray with you?"

"Yes, I guess so. I'll pray with you."

I had listened carefully, but I have to admit—there were still a thousand unanswered questions in my mind.

"Here's the prayer we are going to pray, Carol: 'God, I have been running my own life and have missed the mark you intend for me to hit. Father, thank You for sending Your Son, Jesus Christ, to die for my sins. Thank You for raising Him from the dead and making Him living Lord over all. Come into my heart, Lord Jesus, and begin to reign over my life. Begin to love through me as only You can, and make me a worker in Your vineyard. Amen.'

"Would you like to pray that prayer with me, now?"

"Yes, I would. Do I pray out loud?" I didn't know how this worked, but I wanted to do it right!

"Please repeat after me."

I prayed with the counselor/preacher, but I left his office without believing the prayer would make any difference. I had prayed before, and there hadn't been any difference afterward. I didn't expect this prayer to change me, either.

I drove back to the clinic, excited because I only had to meet with this strange counselor two more times. On the way back, however, I wondered, for the first time, how I would make a living for myself and my children if I were to leave the clinic. I quickly suppressed that thought!

Hit with a Two-by-Four

Upon my return to the clinic, I noticed something was different. From my point of view, women had been dancing in through the front door, singing, "I'm pregnant... Do my abortion..." But when I got back, I saw that all the women coming in the front door were crying. I'd never noticed that before.

I went to the receptionist and the counselors on duty and asked, "What happened while I was gone?"

"Nothing that I know of." The answer was unanimous.

For some reason I was suddenly not comfortable in my normal working environment.

I was saved by the bell—Bell Telephone, that is. It was Harvey. "How are things going, Carol?"

"Everything's great, Harvey. We're having a good day."

It was business as usual with him, and I meant to keep it that way. I couldn't imagine sharing with Harvey what was really happening inside me; I was a bundle of confusion.

I hung up the telephone and continued to stumble around in a daze. Amidst my confusion, Wayne called.

"Wayne, I prayed a prayer with Jack today," I found myself saying. "I suppose I have to leave the clinic, but I don't know what to do." Now, where had those words come from?

"When I find myself in a seemingly impossible situation," Wayne suggested gently, "I just ask God to hit me over the head with a two-by-four."

I closed the door to my office and prayed from the floor of that abortion clinic. "Lord—if there is a Lord—if this is not where you want me to be, hit me over the head with a two-by-four."

I walked out of my office with an inner peace I can't explain. I returned to work thinking, *Perhaps I am to stay in the clinic until I can lead Harvey out of the business. Yes. That's what I must do. I'm supposed to help Harvey get out of this business, too.*

I love Harvey. Two wives loved him, but left him. I can't leave Harvey. No, I have to stay. I have to be loyal to Harvey—he would be loyal to me. I have to lead Harvey out of the abortion business.

We can start opening surgical centers now. We can sell these abortion clinics and use the money to start up. We just have to let this crisis pass. Harvey will see the reasoning behind this move.

Yes, God wants me to help Harvey leave the abortion business. I will join Wayne in working to help Harvey (not Fredi, though—please, God, not Fredi) make peace with God.

I also started taking the women into my office, closing the door, and asking, "Why are you crying?"

One young woman in particular said, "My parents would kill me if they knew I was pregnant."

"No, they wouldn't kill you," I heard myself say. (Wait a minute! This wasn't the way to sell abortions! I should take the fear, amplify it, get their money, and push them through!) As if from a stranger's throat, my voice continued. "Your parents love you. They'll be disappointed, but they'll stand by you. Would you like for me to go home with you to tell your parents?"

This was weird! I was actually looking at the women differently. I wanted to draw close to them and love them.

I thought, *If I don't watch out, I'll be the one leaving the clinic, not Fredi. Or worse—there won't be any women having abortions if I keep helping them, encouraging them to tell their parents, talk to their husbands or boyfriends. If I'm talking people out of abortions, how am I going to make a living? How will I keep my two children in college with their thousand-dollar monthly allowances, new cars, and the rest of it?*

It was business as usual all around me, but certainly not business *inside* me. There was a song in my heart, a joyous song that wasn't there before. It was a song more joyous than any I had known with Tom, more joyous than I experienced as my third child was growing within my womb. The music was within me again—but this time, it was accompanied by love.

I have since learned we must be careful what we ask from God. Laura Randle was God's two-by-four. And I got hit—in all the right places.

So there I was, sitting alone at my dining table, reflecting on the events of the previous twenty-five days. I concluded that the expose wasn't the problem at all. Was my relationship with Harvey the problem? Or was it my relationship with God—perhaps the lack thereof? I had to make a decision about staying with Harvey or getting out. Wayne had just offered me the opportunity to go to Oklahoma and open an abortion clinic, but that was no longer an option. Harvey wanted to do surgical centers, but would he see the value in selling the clinics to open them? Maybe we could open a surgical center for me to run, while he stayed with the abortion clinics?

As I wrestled with my future, Harvey called. "Where were you this morning?"

"I went to church." Then I found myself looking for excuses. "Wayne told me Billie would handle the clinic."

"I expected you to be there today."

Inside me, something clicked. Harvey was making demands and using guilt to motivate me. Well, I wanted no more of that!

"Harvey, when I left yesterday, Wayne told me not to come in, not to worry about it. I took the day off."

"Okay, Carol. Did Wayne talk to you about going to Oklahoma and opening a clinic for us?"

"Yes, he did, Harvey. But I need to sit down with you to talk first."

"Baby, I'm too tired. This is too much. We'll talk later in the week after the television report finishes running."

This would be my last conversation with Harvey as "family" and partner. Harvey and I were finished, in my mind. I began to focus on the future.

What Do I Do Now?

I was scared. Fear gripped me. *When I walk through this door, what'll be on the other side? How am I going to make a living? pay for the cars? the house? the investments? Maybe I'll lose everything—maybe even the children—because the money will be gone. What if all that love I thought they felt for me is tied to money? What if I've tried to buy their love, like Jack said?*

But Wayne promised, in front of Jack, that I would be taken care of. Financially, it would be difficult, but I would have some time to re-adjust. After all, I was promised a one-third partnership in a thriving business. One third of a million-and-a-half dollar business should be worth five hundred thousand dollars in some form. Surely the settlement between us would be no less than two hundred and fifty thousand.

Joe Bob had two more years in college. Kelly had three, but Harvey had said, "Tell Kelly I still want her to work for me. And tell her that no matter what, I'll help her get through school."

I had trusted Harvey Johnson with my dearest secrets and with one of my dearest treasures, my daughter. I let him get close to Kelly and trusted him not to violate her feelings—or her. Now I hoped he would honor his word.

I was initiating an emotional divorce with Harvey. *I won't have to protect him from anyone or anything—not anymore.* I even thought, *I disdain abortion. I hate it. I hate everything about abortion.*

I made arrangements to see my counselor Monday morning at 9 A.M.

"Jack," I told him, "I've made the decision not to go to Oklahoma. I've also decided I don't want to work with Harvey anymore. I need to regroup my life and start over. I want to reach a settlement with Harvey. The minimum I'll settle for is two hundred and fifty thousand dollars in payment for my one-third interest."

"Carol, let me talk to Wayne and see what their position is. Unfortunately, I'm sure we haven't heard the last about what they'll try to do."

"It looks that way," I agreed. "Harvey is really acting strangely. Last night he wouldn't meet with me. I'd bet he's going to protect himself from me by using Wayne as his shield."

"I suspect you're right, Carol," Jack said.

"What do you think I should do?"

"What about the Promenade Meat Center?" he asked.

"It's in a mess right now."

"Does it have the potential to provide you with a living?"

"I'm not sure."

"Carol, I think you ought to concentrate on getting the butcher shop in order while I try to work things out with Wayne."

"I'm going to the clinic to clean out my desk, tell everyone goodbye, and close that door in my life."

"I know that won't be easy for you to do."

"I'll call you later and let you know how it went."

I got to the clinic about eleven o'clock and stumbled around as if I were lost. Billie and I went to lunch, as usual for a Monday. "Billie," I confided, "this is my last day."

"What do you mean, Carol?"

"I've decided I'm getting out of the abortion business."

"What are you going to do?"

"Run my butcher shop, I guess. I don't know."

When we got back to the clinic, I pulled my car to the back and slowly started to clear my desk. It felt really strange being there. The employees kept asking me operational questions, even though Billie was now in charge. I wanted to get out of there and go home.

At about four in the afternoon, I bade farewell to all the employees, through many tears.

They kept asking, "Why are you leaving, Carol?"

My only answer was, "Because I'm supposed to."

Without fanfare or final applause, the Scarlet Lady, who dreamed of being the leading lady in the abortion industry, walked out of the clinic. It was twenty-seven days after her strange counselor told her, "Someone is going to be leaving the clinic within the next thirty days."

It wasn't Fredi, after all.

On Monday evening, the expose aired for the fourth night. I watched as Channel 4 interviewed women who'd had problems with the clinic. I had problems with it too, problems of a different kind. I hated to see myself aligned with abortionists; it already seemed like another person, another life.

The deep inner peace I felt was still overriding the storm surrounding me. The children seemed to share my calm, as if they, too, were relieved.

On Tuesday morning, Kelly went to work at the clinic. At about ten, she called. "Mom, I can't stand this place. Do I have to stay? Do I have to keep working here?"

"No, baby. Quit and come home. I'll call Harvey and tell him you aren't going to work there anymore." Kelly was relieved and so was I.

I thought, *There will be no ties—no ties at all with the abortion business—as soon as I call Harvey.* I dialed his office. "This is Carol. I'd like to speak to Harvey."

"He isn't in today."

I called his home and Fredi answered.

"Is Harvey in?"

"Carol, he can't talk to you now."

"Fredi, could he—or could both of you—meet me for lunch?"

"Harvey is too upset today, Carol. He'll call you."

The corporate attorney called, instead. "Can you come over to my office to go over a few things at about four this afternoon?" he asked.

At 4 P.M. I walked into the attorney's office. Two attorneys questioned me about the "complications" (botched abortions) I was involved in and what I knew about them. I knew they wanted to see how much I knew—how much damage I could do if Harvey and I didn't come to a resolution.

I related the names and details of fourteen botched abortions, mostly abortions performed by J. Harvey Johnson, M.D.

A few minutes after I got home, the telephone rang. "Carol, this is Billie. I wanted to tell you I just wrote a letter, firing you. Harvey called me and told me what to say and told me to sign it. I'm sorry. I wanted you to hear it from me."

"Fired? You can't fire a partner! Is this how he's going to do it?"

"I'm sorry, Carol."

"Thanks, Billie. I'll talk to you later."

I called Harvey at home again and demanded that Fredi let me talk to him. When he came on the line he said, "I'm sorry, Carol." Not "Hello"—just "I'm sorry, Carol."

"So this is the way you intend to treat me after all we've been through together? This is how you treat 'family'? We'll see about that! Goodbye." I slammed down the receiver.

I was disgusted at myself for ever trusting such a man, but I was also oddly relieved. He had abandoned me—but I hadn't deserted him.

It was truly over. But now, how was I going to make a living?

I quickly called Jack Shaw and told him all that had transpired throughout the day.

"Carol, meet Gwen and me at 9 tonight at the Denny's at I-635 and Preston Road."

"Thanks, Jack. I'll see you at 9." The last segment of the expose aired at 10, but I didn't care. I had to get my agreement worked out fast and get on with my life.

I met Jack and his wife Gwen at Denny's, right on schedule. I had met Gwen at church. She seemed to be such a lovely woman. I usually tried hard not to swear around her, but under the present circumstances it was very difficult to refrain.

"Jack, did you talk to Wayne today?" I asked.

"Yes, I did. But he's not saying much."

"Well, I'm not going to settle for one (blankety-blank) penny less than two hundred and fifty thousand dollars. The appraisal on the two clinics came back at one million, five hundred thousand dollars."

"Yes, but those were done for insurance purposes. Wayne had it done; that's just a rough estimate. And it was done for you to be able to buy out Fredi."

"Even with exaggerated appraisals, Jack, a one-third interest in the business should bring two hundred and fifty thousand dollars," I insisted.

Jack looked me in the eye. "Carol, you'll be lucky to get one hundred and twenty-five thousand. There's been no stock issued. Do you have anything in writing?"

"No, nothing," I admitted. I had trusted Harvey completely. He was supposed to have been redrafting his will and realigning his business affairs before he issued the stock. "But what about the insurance policy?" I asked. "I know it was issued. I signed the check myself."

"Wayne told me the insurance policy was never issued because of all the problems between you and Fredi."

For the first time since we had prayed together, I was scared and depressed. Everything was out of control. I had been whipped and had no money.

"Jack, what am I going to do?" I whispered.

"Just go back to the butcher shop and work. I'll get with Wayne and put this situation to bed. Don't worry. It'll be all right." I don't know why I believed this man was any different than all the others who had lied to me, but I took comfort in his confidence.

The butcher shop was really in a mess, more than I could have imagined. I called Ibrahim to confront him. "Are you going to help me with this mess and come up with your part of the money?"

All I could get him to agree to do was take over a house in Garland that we had bought together. Thank God for small favors. At least Ibrahim was out of my life.

Joe Bob called Fredi. "I won't be mowing your lawn anymore," he told her.

"Why, Joe Bob? Keeping our lawn has nothing to do with your mother's situation," she whined.

"It does to me. I won't do business with anyone who treats my mother like Harvey has." Yeah, Joe Bob!

On Friday, Wayne called. "Carol, some of the employees are quitting. Would you come out for a few minutes Saturday to help calm things down?"

"Yes, Wayne. I'll be there."

My presence was all Wayne wanted.

"Why did you leave, Carol?" the employees asked me, over and over. "What happened wasn't your fault."

Wayne didn't want me to answer any questions. I listened as Jan, Harvey's daughter, kept telling everyone her father's perspective on the situation. I actually didn't need to say anything. The employees knew better than anyone what was going on in the clinic.

But they didn't know what was going on inside me, and I couldn't tell them.

After the meeting, Wayne took me back to the office and handed me the checkbook. "Write yourself a check for twelve thousand dollars."

I wrote the check and left, taking it to the bank on Monday morning to get a cashier's check—just to be sure Wayne didn't stop payment on it.

Jack called on Tuesday morning. "Carol, can you meet with Wayne, Harvey and me tonight at 8 at the Regency Hotel?"

"What's going on?"

"Hopefully, we can get everything ironed out tonight."

"I'll be there." This I had to see.

I'd been waiting to see Harvey Johnson, face to face. Originally, I wanted to tell him why I left the clinic, about what was going on in my life with the Lord. Now, I was too hurt and angry to talk about that. He was going to get the full load—from point-blank range.

I figured Harvey would be sugar-sweet and try to get me to back down on my implied threats. Instead, he was direct—and angry. "Why didn't you tell me about the butcher shop?"

"I didn't want you to think it would hurt my work at the clinic."

I was taken aback by Harvey's anger over my secrecy about the butcher shop. Did he think he owned me?

Throughout the meeting, Harvey wouldn't meet my eyes. I assumed that meant he knew how angry I was.

"Harvey, I've trusted you completely," I told him. "You know very well that one-third of the business is mine. Tom warned me to get it in writing, but I said, 'No. Harvey would never abuse me.' You know I've worked like a dog to build our business, and now you say it wasn't 'our' business. How can you live with yourself?"

He was still silent. He was just like all the rest of the men in my life—weak! When it came to fulfilling his part of the bargain, forget it!

"And what about your promise to Kelly?" I continued. "I guess you've forgotten that, too. I helped you build the clinic business. Now you can help me build the butcher shop. Don't you think that's fair, Harvey?"

"Yes, Carol. I guess it is," he mumbled.

The tension was so high that Jack interceded. "We need to stop this meeting. Let Wayne and me work out something between you two. Let's call it a night."

I left the meeting, pleased to some extent. At least Harvey knew how angry I was at him. I hated him—or did I really hate myself for loving and trusting him?

As I drove home that evening, I thought, *One thing is clear: Avoiding sex with a man doesn't mean you won't get hurt by him. I guess I can't have any kind of relationship without being hurt.*

Jack met with Wayne to work out a settlement. After several days, he called. "Carol, I believe I have a settlement we can live with."

We met and discussed the details.

"Carol, they're willing to pay you a total of seventy-two thousand dollars. You wrote yourself a twelve-thousand dollar check at the office. The remaining sixty thousand will be paid in monthly installments of five thousand dollars for twelve months."

"How do I know they'll pay me in full?" I questioned.

"I'll have them draft a personal note and have Harvey sign it. Everything will be in writing," he promised.

"That's not even half as much as I hoped I'd get. Maybe we should sue them and let everything come out in the open."

"Honestly, Carol, that would be very expensive and time-consuming. I think you need to get on with your life," he advised.

"Jack, five thousand dollars is not nearly enough to meet my needs, with two kids in college. I won't be able to pay my bills. I could lose everything."

"I know, Carol, and I can't promise that you won't. You're going to have to make some big adjustments in your lifestyle."

I'm going to have to make some big adjustments in my lifestyle? What does he think I've been doing—ever since that first prayer?

"I understand, Jack," I said, hesitantly. "I guess if you think this is the best we can do, then I'll accept it. But they'd better pay like they've promised."

"I'll call Wayne and tell him to draw up the necessary papers. Everything will work out for the best. You'll see—in time."

But how much time was left?

13

....

JOURNEY THROUGH
THE WILDERNESS

I WALKED OUT of the abortion industry carrying a lot more baggage than when I'd entered. But I now had new strength to carry the extra weight, and new friends to help me unload the baggage I didn't need to carry anymore.

I had mountains of debt from foolish spending and a budget requirement far exceeding five thousand dollars a month. I had a taste for the power of money and for "the good life." I had the added guilt of the 35,000 abortions I had sold, plus my own. But, also in my baggage was the knowledge of the prayers I had prayed—those with Jack and those alone on the floor of the abortion clinic. And I had firsthand knowledge of the swiftness of God's two-by-four.

A lot of old tapes were playing in my head, tapes from my past that beckoned me to return to my old life. Now I faced new challenges without the tools I was accustomed to. And the new people in my life were nothing like those I had been around all my life. It was as if I had died, and awakened living somewhere else.

I think of it as my wilderness time, because it was a time of wandering about aimlessly (so it seemed to me) and seeing little rationale for why I had to endure all I was enduring. I didn't understand the changes that had to take place in me—thoughts, attitudes, actions, desires, values, motives—in order for the real me to be born.

Even today, I am not anywhere near who I intend to be, but I'm grateful for tolerance from others as I am transformed into a new person. I wish everyone could experience the type of understanding I've received from those around me who love me for who I am, not what I do for them. In fact, when I do fall into my old, habitual patterns of jealousy, assertiveness, and competitiveness, they look inside my heart and see that I don't mean to be hurtful—even when I am.

The Transformation Process

A butcher shop, of all places, was the first station in my wilderness journey. I find that ironic. My father introduced me to a butcher shop and the slaughtering of animals when I was only two. The abortion clinic was the butcher shop I chose in my other life.

At least The Promenade Meat Center was a butcher shop that sustained life, rather than snuffing out life.

God provided places of refuge and refreshment in my wilderness journey. The spiritual baggage I carried from being in the abortion business weighed heavily on me. I was out of the abortion industry, but not out from under the guilt of those 35,001 abortions. I felt as though a big, conspicuous "A" was emblazoned on my forehead, especially when I walked into church.

But somehow, although I felt awkward, I got involved in the church as much as I could. The people were warm and loving, just like my pastor, Jack Shaw.

I couldn't figure it out. What was their angle? Sooner or later, I knew it would surface. I was much more suspicious of them than they ever thought of being toward me.

I began to enjoy using the Bible as a guide. The day I walked out of the clinic I started having a devotional time, reading two chapters of the Bible every morning. Prayer became more and more important in my daily life. I screamed out in desperation several times a day and the answers were always there (although sometimes it took me a while to see them).

When Jack first told me he was a preacher, I became defensive about abortion, intent on justifying my occupation. But as we spent more time together, I began to say to him, "I'm not certain abortion is wrong."

Rather than argue with me, he always replied, "Carol, take one day at a time and pray, 'Lord, whatever is in my life You want to take out or change, help me to recognize it and cooperate with You.'" He always prayed, "Lord, show Carol the truth. Let her see any deception in her life that You want her to be free from." He never condemned me!

I should have known, after our first prayer together, not to pray with Jack unless I expected an answer. It was just a matter of time until God would reveal His Word on the subject of abortion. Deep inside, I longed to know the truth about abortion and its effects on my life. I longed to be free from the weight of my own secret abortion. I wanted to confess my secret to Jack so many times, but I couldn't.

Nelson and Stephanie Cook were God's special gifts to me, helping me come to grips with facing little children, infants, and their parents. They would invite me into their home for dinner and let me baby-sit with the only child they had at that time.

Stephanie told me about the difficult time she had getting pregnant. Of course, with my abortionist's history, I could have felt terrible. But the atmosphere was so full of love, so free of condemnation. I really needed that. I also needed to be entrusted with the care of their daughter to know that they had confidence in me and loved me unconditionally.

Stephanie was a committed Christian who discipled me in many ways. I began to feel like a woman again. I even developed maternal feelings, without the guilt which so often had been the backdrop for my relationship with my own children. And their little girl, Kimberly, was so beautiful and loving. In all of these relationships, God was breaking down walls within me.

Jack encouraged me to write my testimony and prayerfully look for an opportunity to share it. I really got into the project, eager to see what would happen. I wondered if God could use me to help someone else.

In the butcher shop, I waited for the opportunity to tell someone about my newfound faith. One day, a young man came in and introduced himself. "Hi. I'm Ron Henderson. I own the company that washes your windows. It's time to collect for the month."

"How much do I owe you?" I asked.

"Ten dollars."

"Here you go," I said, handing him the money. "I haven't seen you washing our windows."

"No. I'm a seminary student, and I don't have time to wash the windows. I do the administrative work."

"A seminary student! I've just become a Christian!" I exclaimed.

"Good for you."

"I'd like to share what happened to me. I'm learning how to give my testimony. Do you have five minutes?"

"No, I'm sorry, I'm in a hurry today. Maybe next month."

I thought little about Ron Henderson until about a month later, when he came by to collect another ten dollars for the month's window washing. "Carol, do you have time to share that testimony with me?" he asked.

"Yes. I surely do." I related the story of my involvement in the abortion industry, about Jesus Christ finding me there, and my invitation to Him to be my Lord and Savior. I talked about God's sense of humor. "Just look where He put me—in a different kind of butcher shop!"

"Carol, I thought you were going to tell me another dry conversion story," Ron beamed, "but this is truly a miracle! Thanks for sharing it with me."

I visited with Ron from month to month when he came to collect his money. In God's time, my eagerness to share with Ron and his faithfulness to follow up with me proved to be very significant.

When I was involved with church activities and my new friends, things went great. But sometimes, my old friends from the abortion clinic dropped by the butcher shop. I didn't know what to say. I didn't want to talk about the clinic, but I didn't feel as if I could really share my new situation with them. After all…how could they understand it if I didn't?

When they'd leave, I'd really struggle with my thoughts and emotions. It was like I flipped a switch, and the old me started reciting the old stuff—those old tapes. *The life I so carefully planned and built is gone. The hurt is still here. The pain is unbearable.*

Why wasn't I happy with two clinics? Why couldn't I be satisfied? But, no. I wanted to be a millionaire. None of this would be happening if I hadn't tried to work things out with Fredi so we could expand.

The counselor was supposed to solve the problem, work out the problem between Fredi and me. He said someone would be leaving the clinic within thirty days. I never dreamed it would be me.

Then the old stuff would switch off and new stuff would play in my mind again. *The prayer did make some kind of difference in my life. I do feel some kind of peace that I can't really explain. I don't want to go back to the abortion business. I don't want to be involved with someone like Harvey anymore.*

Poor Harvey. I really worked him over in my mind when the old tapes played. *Harvey emotionally raped me. Harvey helped me kill my baby. Harvey was the authority figure I turned to for rescue. But, he didn't rescue me. He helped me kill my baby instead.*

I hate him. I hate him because he didn't act the part of a good physician. I hate him because he gave me the "easy" way out. He helped ruin my life and my marriage. He killed my baby!

My mind would wander down the "old life" trail for a while longer. Then it would shift back to the "new life" track.

My life is changed now, and I will never go back to that other life. As tough as things are—and there are times when I don't think I'm going to survive—even the worst on this side is better than the best on the abortion side.

Just being able to sleep at night, knowing I didn't kill any babies that day, is a relief. I don't have to worry about the baby that was too big to go down the disposal, about it being found in the trash can. I don't have that cold feeling anymore.

The changes in my life were good, despite the constant emotional turmoil. I worked all day, went home, cooked a steak from the butcher shop, made a salad, watched television, and dropped into bed, exhausted from the day's work. I remember resting like never before. I started to feel better than I had in many years.

My father tried his best to help. "Sister, you'd better get married while you can. You're getting too old to wait much longer."

Gee, thanks, Daddy! Bless his heart, he was concerned, I guess.

I tried turning to Tom, my ex-husband and frequent advisor. He came by the butcher shop one time, but that was it—no more. I should have known Tom couldn't provide the emotional stability I needed to navigate my wilderness.

Adventures in the Pits

In November, my personal financial picture really took a downturn. Harvey cut off his payments, as I knew he would. He made the first twelve-thousand-dollar payment and two five-thousand-dollar payments, then quit. I called Jack. "Just as I suspected, Harvey isn't going to honor his agreement."

"Yes, he will, Carol. He'll honor the note payment or we'll seek legal remedy. I'll call Wayne and get back with you."

"I've seen Wayne work before," I warned. "He's going to blame me, because the business is down. He'll claim I'm the cause of the poor cash flow, but his management style is the cause. Just be prepared."

"You may be right, Carol."

Sure enough, Wayne filled Jack's ears with my failures as a business manager and with how much I had cost the clinic. Jack kept telling me, "Carol, it'll work out. We'll get you the money."

I will never forget standing next to those coolers in the butcher shop, screaming at God, kicking the coolers. No one was there except God and me. Yes, I could feel Him try to comfort me, but I couldn't understand it at the time. I just kept screaming, for weeks and weeks. Harvey's latest action hurt me deeply.

Now, at the lowest point in my life, abortionists started calling me, asking me to go to work with them.

The abortionist/psychiatrist from the clinic, Dr. Miller, came by the butcher shop to talk to me about setting up a new clinic near Prestonwood Mall. His idea was for the patients to be able to shop while they waited for their abortion. The clinic would give them a beeper and signal them when it was time for their abortion. I thought it was a novel idea, especially coming from him.

Another abortionist from New York wined and dined me in a similar vein. He offered me an arrangement like the one I had with Harvey. Dr. Stein thought the way to get me to work with him was to have an affair with me. That made me sick. He only thought of me as a weak woman, not a potential partner. I almost laughed in his face.

From a strictly financial point of view, the timing was perfect for me to go back into the abortion business. I was about to go crazy over my financial crisis. I was at the end of myself, viewing all my past mistakes and how brutally they had affected my life and my children. But I desperately needed money.

Dr. Stein suggested I convert to the Jewish faith. He explained, "Jews believe that life begins at birth. You can do abortions with no qualms in my religion."

I treasured my new faith, however, and hated the killing business. It was a difficult decision, turning down each effort of the abortionists to re-enlist me. But somehow, I managed to avoid falling into those pits.

Financially, I was in a pickle. Without the five thousand dollars coming in from Harvey, things really got bleak in a hurry. I called Jack continuously. "Have you heard anything from Wayne?" I'd ask.

"Yes. He tells me he's trying to resolve everything. It's evident to me he signed the note, against Harvey's lawyer's advice. We'll get it worked out," he always assured me.

"I hope so. I don't know how much longer I can hold out at the butcher shop. Harvey agreed to help me during this time."

"I know, Carol. It'll get resolved."

At the butcher shop, we went from one crisis to another. I was constantly screaming, "God, why? Where is the money going to come from this time?" The more financial pressure I endured, the more I was tempted to go back into the abortion business. But I chose to tighten my belt and hold on.

The first of those things to go—things I bought with the "blood" money from the abortion industry—was my Toronado. I got angry, at first, with God. I sold it to help take care of some of the immediate bills and to relieve the monthly outgo during the first month Harvey failed to pay me.

I cried out to God. I didn't understand why it hurt when old things fall away. I felt alone, downtrodden, as if I had no friends in the world. My old mental tapes assured me I had self-destructed a situation that was perfect. I had a good working relationship with Harvey, without sex. I could support my children and pay their way through college. Everything was going perfectly. But I'd blown it, and there was nowhere to go. I was stuck in the butcher shop.

The emotional and spiritual struggle intensified. Jack was there every step of the way, either talking to me on the telephone or spending a few minutes with me daily—discipling me, feeding me a solid diet of Scripture. He constantly showed me how to live the Christian life.

I didn't trust myself with any decision. I called Jack or Gwen constantly with the crisis of the day, because I needed help from someone competent and trustworthy. They answered my questions with paraphrased scriptures, teaching me how to use my new Christian principles in everyday life. I didn't understand that they were using Scripture at the time, but the answer always made sense.

"Jack, what am I going to do about all the bills? The vendors are calling me constantly, wanting to be paid."

"Carol, you have to be honest with them and tell them your situation and what you intend to do. Offer to return their merchandise if they want you to. You're operating under grace with them," he reminded me patiently.

"Try to see things from their point of view, but don't take responsibility for their business decisions. You didn't sell you the merchandise—they did. They're trying to pressure you because of their own mistakes. They should have known that you'd be a 'slow pay' account; you weren't a choice account to begin with. Relax, and put your marketing skills to work."

"What about the lease payment?"

"Call the landlord and be honest with him. Tell him what you found when you came in, how far behind you are. See if you can defer the rent payments for ninety days, moving them to the end of the lease. If the location isn't good, time will prove that. Look at the empty space around you. Find out how the other tenants are doing. Go to the shopping center merchant's association meeting. Get on top of the facts about the traffic. Market, Carol. Get creative with ways to package your merchandise."

"What about the bank loan interest payment?"

"Go see them, too. But get a handle on the accounts payable first. Then go to the bank and update them. Ask them to work with you."

As the financial pressure mounted, I discovered the difference between "needs" and "wants." All of my "needs" were met—yes, later than I would have wanted—but they were met. I prayed for patience one time, and an older Christian cautioned me, "Oh, don't pray for patience because you'll get it. It's just that the way it comes will be painful."

I was starting to learn about waiting on the Lord.

On one occasion, when things were particularly bad, Kelly was with me in the butcher shop. The electricity was scheduled to be cut off at 5:00 P.M. I prayed about the need and was at peace with the situation.

Kelly didn't understand the change in me. She just knew we'd be out of business if the electricity was cut off, and she was watching me. Finally she asked, "Why aren't you going crazy?"

I had the opportunity to tell her, "The Lord will meet our need."

What an amazing answer it was when a new Christian friend of mine, a man Kelly didn't know, walked in and tried to give me more money than we needed! Now, I'm not suggesting it happened that way every time; but it did seem to happen when I really needed it.

Each need was met in God's timing, not mine. I was tested, and after a few months I realized I was starting to trust God to meet my needs. Sometimes the need was met by a new Christian friend who would call to say, "I have something for you, Carol. I'll be by shortly." They'd come by with cash or a check in hand.

I found out I didn't need a tax shelter. The condominium in Houston was the next "blood money" thing to go. They started foreclosure proceedings in November, ending with foreclosure in January. One by one, I watched each of the possessions bought with tainted money slip away. Not all at once, but gradually, the Lord purged my life of all those things.

In time, my financial problem became clear to me—how do I manage this monster I have created, rather than blaming God for not letting me hold on to it?

The children could live on less than a thousand dollars a month in college, I decided. Somehow, I could pay for the two sports cars. The apartment in Oak Cliff was manageable. God would help me take care of my living expenses. The butcher shop would either make it, or it wouldn't.

Christmas was slim under our tree, but it was very warm in my heart. We celebrated the true meaning of Christmas for the first time. Even the "recycled" gifts were given gratefully to the people I loved.

I thought my wilderness journey was over, but it had only entered a second phase. There was much more to come. But the new pitfalls were different—just the opposite of what I expected.

Beware Lest You Fall

In January, 1984, Jack introduced me to a shopping center developer who hired me to work in his restaurant division. Suddenly, I was introduced to a true "high roller" lifestyle, with all the trimmings.

I agreed to work for a salary of five thousand dollars a month, which was an adjustment. My first assignment was to get a job with a major sandwich shop, learning the way they operated their business. I went to a store near the butcher shop so it would be easy to run back and forth. I'll never forget applying for that job. I don't know who was more shocked: the girl behind the counter or her young black manager.

We walked through the kitchen to his office. "Why do you want to work here?" he asked.

I explained, "I have just lost my income, and quite frankly, I can use the money. I'd like to work the noon shift so I can have evenings off."

"That's the shift I have trouble filling. I can only pay you $4.25 per hour," he apologized.

"That's fine."

"Can you start at eleven o'clock tomorrow?"

"I'll be here. Thank you."

The relationship between the young manager and me was very close. He sensed something different in me, the smell of something he had not been around, and he wanted that something. Little did he know it was the Lord—and I was just getting to know Him myself.

I'd been working at the sandwich shop a couple of weeks when my boss, the developer, called. "Carol, I've just finished the lease on our first restaurant site. Can you come by the office late this afternoon to sign it?"

"Sure, I'll be there."

The environment, the champagne, the attention he turned on me was overwhelming. Part of me desperately wanted it all—the powerful corporate man with a plane that could whisk me away. Part of me knew that it was wrong. I was scared. I had to find a way to say 'no'. I had done it before; I could do it again—couldn't I?

I failed the test.

I continued to work at the sandwich shop until May. I moved to the corporate offices, just before the ICSC (International Convention of Shopping Centers) convention, held in Las Vegas. From Las Vegas it was off to Chicago, the Florida Keys, Santa Fe—all on his private plane. I watched as tens of thousands of dollars were spent on frivolities.

It reminded me of myself, but I was a rank amateur compared to the crowd I was now traveling with. Even Harvey couldn't compare. It was all too much for a little old country girl. This man could talk the Christian lingo, but he didn't live it.

I began to understand there are two kinds of Christians: those who talk it (including me, in those days) and who use Christianity as a tool, and those who have a real heartfelt desire to please the Lord. Finally, I began to learn to separate the two.

What an awful dilemma. I had heard about "hypocrites," but now I felt like their queen. Every time I got around Jack or was in church, I felt awful. Thank God, I did not run from that place of refuge and refreshment. I continued my church activities and daily Bible study, looking for a way out.

God didn't abandon me. One Sunday morning Gordon Werner, a deacon at the church, offered some thoughts from Psalm 139. In my devotional time I turned to it and read for the first time: "For You did form my inward parts, You did knit me together in my mother's womb" (verse 13). I was convinced I had been killing babies. The words that really got me were these: "Your eyes saw my unformed substance, and in Your book all the days of my life were written, before they ever took shape, when as yet there was none of them." (verse 16).

I remembered holding those little babies' bodies in my hand as I cleaned the instruments. I specifically remembered that each of them had intestines—yes, some threadlike—but, they all had intestines. I remembered wondering why God gave them intestines if He knew they were going to be aborted.

I knew now God intended for each of the 35,001 babies to live, each one that I had helped abort.

The weight of my sin became very heavy, but I remembered 1 John 1:9: "If we [freely] admit that we have sinned and confess our sins, He is faithful and just [true to His own nature and promises] and will forgive us our sins (dismiss our lawlessness)." And now, the part I love: "and continuously cleanse us from all unrighteousness—everything not in conformity to His will in purpose, thought and action."

It took a little while, but Jack's prayer finally worked. I knew abortion was not only wrong, but a terrible sin against God. The sin could be forgiven and I could be cleansed, however. I began to believe the big "A" emblazoned on my forehead could be removed.

I became pro-life. I asked God, "What am I going to do?" I was in a stew. I wasn't in a spiritual position to reach out with my newfound truth because of my hypocrisy. And besides, I was afraid of becoming a pro-lifer because I had viewed pro-lifers as angry, violent people—not because I knew any of them, but because of the press. They certainly were not portrayed as kind, loving people.

Emerging from the Wilderness

I continued to wander through my wilderness, but not alone. Now I prayed, "God, please help me out of this situation." I did *not* ask to be hit over the head with a two-by-four! Gradually, I began to feel stronger. The time came when I refused to play the game any longer with my boss.

At the same time, God hit the developer over the head with a two-by-four. I guess he must have prayed with someone, too. In September, I was one of fifty-one people released from his company.

During my time with the developer, I was offered all the things of the world that I thought would make me happy. I could and did try it all, but it left me empty.

I went back to the butcher shop again. Just when I thought it couldn't get any worse, Jack announced, "Carol, you're going to have to file suit against Harvey. Let's use the courts to collect the note."

"Okay, Jack. I knew it would come down to this sooner or later. I haven't been paid anything in a year. Why should I expect anything now?"

I called my lawyer and told him to proceed with the suit. I was prepared to tell everything in the courtroom if I had to. I surprised myself by being able to leave the battle with Harvey to the legal system, keeping it off a personal level.

The butcher shop was a losing proposition; I prayed to get out. A buyer came along in November, and we made arrangements with the bank for him to assume the note, with me remaining as a guarantor. The buyer agreed to pay me five thousand dollars for my equity.

On the day we were to close the deal, the health department came in and threatened to shut us down if the floor wasn't redone. The purchasers backed out because of the added expense. In a panic, I tried to call Jack at the office.

"He's out right now," I was told. "I don't know when he'll be back. Is this Carol?"

"Yes," I tearfully replied.

"This is Jerry. Are you all right?"

"As good as I can be. The deal to sell the butcher shop just fell through because the health department is about to close the place. Ask Jack to call if you talk to him."

"I will."

In what seemed like just a few minutes, I looked up to see Jerry Green and Richard Bowles, two men from my church, walking in the front door. I rushed out to meet them. Both of them gave me a big hug.

We talked over the situation, then they prayed with me. I called the buyers and offered to forego the five-thousand-dollar equity payment if they would go ahead and close the deal. They agreed.

"What are you going to do when you get out of here?" Richard asked.

"I don't know."

"Call me as soon as you're finished here."

"I will. Thank you both for everything."

As soon as I knew when I would be finished at the butcher shop, I called Richard. "What do you have in mind?"

"We need someone to handle our leasing. Are you interested?"

"I sure am."

The day I walked out of the butcher shop and went to work for Jerry and Richard at Bowles/Green, a real estate development company, I walked out of my wilderness. These two men were a breath of fresh air. The day I went to work with them, Richard said, "Carol, you're only with us until God moves you into full-time work."

"Full-time work? What do you mean?"

"A work for God."

I thought, *He's crazy.* But by now, I should have known better. I felt good; I was out of my wilderness and on my way into a new, fulfilling life. My wilderness journey had been rough. But I felt so protected and loved, even amid my pratfalls. I felt a special attachment to the Lord. He loved me enough for me to care for me while I learned to walk with Him, even when I stumbled.

I would discover that I was only beginning my walk with the Lord.

14

....

PLAYING FOR THE
OTHER TEAM

I'D BEEN WORKING for Jerry and Richard a few months when Ron Henderson called. "Carol? This is Ron—Ron Henderson. My company washed your windows at the butcher shop."

"Yes, Ron. I remember you."

"I'm now on staff with the Dallas Right to Life organization, and we've been praying for God to send someone to help us, someone who has first-hand experience in the abortion industry. Would you be willing to talk with us?"

"Yes, I'll talk to them—but Jack Shaw, the man who led me to Christ, will have to be in the meeting."

"That won't be a problem. Bill Price will be calling you to set up the meeting. Thanks, Carol."

I hung up the telephone and thought, *God doesn't miss a trick! He uses the weakest attempts on our part to accomplish His work.* My first five-minute testimony to a seminary student was about to bear God's fruit.

The next day, Bill Price called. "Carol, this is Bill Price with Greater Dallas Right to Life. Ron Henderson told you I would be calling, didn't he?"

"Yes."

"We're working on pro-life legislation for Texas, and we'd like to meet with you to see if you could help us testify before the legislature." I couldn't believe it!

We set up an early morning appointment the next week. I contacted Jack to make sure he could be at the meeting. "Jack, I'm scared of what they'll do, the pro-choicers; even the pro-lifers! And I'm scared of what might happen if I tell the whole truth. I'm not worried about being sued by Harvey. But what about Sheryl's death and all those other botched abortions?"

179

"Whom are you going to trust, Carol—God or man?" That was just like Jack—he always made it sound so simple.

"God, I guess."

It was time for prayer, prayer, and more prayer. *God, is this what you want me to do? What will happen to my children? To me? This could be dangerous.* I kept quoting the Scripture to myself, "For God did not give us a spirit of timidity—of cowardice, of craven and cringing and fawning fear—but [He has given us a spirit] of power and of love and of calm and well-balanced mind and discipline and self-control (2 Timothy 1:7).

Our first meeting was cancelled due to snow and ice. We rescheduled, and I prayed some more. When the ice and snow melted, Bill Price, Curtis Brown (the attorney who had drawn up the proposed legislation), Jack and I had our meeting. After formal introductions we proceeded to evaluate the possibility of my helping them.

"Bill, Jack will help me make my final decision about working with you and Curtis," I told him. "I know how important the bill is to you, but I'm really hesitant to get involved right now."

"I understand, Carol. But let me explain what we're trying to do..."

When Bill and Curtis finished, Jack said, "Bill, you cannot sensationalize Carol's involvement in this cause."

"We wouldn't do that."

Curtis continued, "We need to get an affidavit, Carol. Would you tell me everything you can about your experience in the abortion industry?"

I kept it pretty shallow, but they were very excited.

When we finished the meeting, three hours later, Curtis said, "I'll go back and finish your affidavit and send it back to you for review. If you and Jack are satisfied with it, please sign it and return it to me."

After the meeting I was numb, but very joyful inside. *So this is what I'm supposed to do with my life. Maybe Richard was right.* His words, "You're only with us until God moves you into full-time work," rang in my ears.

I tried to keep my mind on my work until the affidavit came. When it was delivered, Jack and I read it. Then we sent it to Ed Blackstone, my attorney. All three of us made a few changes, and I sent it back to Curtis Brown. He incorporated our changes and sent it back for my signature.

Fear Not

I remember standing in front of that notary public, thinking, *How can this be me? I am going to Austin to testify for a pro-life bill as a pro-lifer, not as a pro-choicer.*

Somehow, the pro-life community heard about me and began to ask me to speak, but Right to Life wanted me to be a surprise witness in Austin. They asked me not to do any pro-life speaking engagements before the legislative hearings.

I anxiously awaited a phone call concerning the date of the hearings. It finally came: I would testify on Monday, April 15th, 1985.

I immediately informed the prayer chain at the church and my north Dallas Bible study group. They began to pray that God would use me as His instrument.

On Sunday night, April 14, I spoke publicly as a pro-lifer for the first time—at my church. The attendance was unbelievable (and we didn't even serve food). They came to hear me and pray for me.

I stumbled through my testimony as best I could, fighting my tears and fears. When I finished, Jack asked me to remain in front while the church leaders and members surrounded me at the altar to pray with me. It was a very special time.

I don't know what I expected, but when I left the church, my spirit was soaring. I felt very strong.

The next morning I flew to Austin. When I entered the Capitol building, I walked right into my old friends, the pro-choicers. I felt the anger and oppression seething in them, feelings I hadn't experienced since the day I left the abortion clinic. I heard their angry questions; "Who's going to speak first?" I rushed past them to join the pro-lifers.

We went inside the room where the hearing was to take place and ran into angry, boisterous pro-choicers. I could feel the weight of evil, pressing on my spirit even more strongly. I grabbed my things and rushed outside to talk to God for a while.

I sat down on a big rock near the Reagan building in the morning sun. The strength I felt the night before was already sapped. I wasn't nearly as prepared to fight in God's battle as I thought. I began to cry out to God for help.

Lord, I know You can zap those abortion clinics. I've read about Your power in the Bible, and I've felt your two-by-four. Why don't you just zap the abortion clinics, and let me go on with my life?

At that point in my Christian walk, I did not read the Old Testament. I didn't like the law or legalism I thought I'd find there. I loved the grace and mercy of the New Testament. I even had my personal Bible trained. All the Old Testament pages were stuck together, and the Book just naturally opened to the New Testament.

But my dog had chewed up my Bible. I had Kelly's new, untrained, Amplified Bible with me. It didn't know it wasn't supposed to open to the Old Testament. It opened to the book of Isaiah:

> You whom I [the Lord] have taken from the ends of the earth and have called from the corners of it, and said to you, You are My servant—I have chosen you and not cast you off [even though you are exiled].
>
> Fear not [there is nothing to fear], for I am with you; do not look around you in terror and be dismayed, for I am your God. I will strengthen and harden you to difficulties; yes, I will help you; yes, I will hold you up and retain you with My [victorious] right hand of rightness and justice.
>
> Behold, all they who are enraged and inflamed against you shall be put to shame and confounded; they who strive against you shall be as nothing and shall perish.
>
> You shall seek those who contend with you, but shall not find them; they who war against you shall be as nothing, as nothing at all.
>
> For I the Lord your God hold your right hand; I am the Lord, Who says to you, Fear not; I will help you!
>
> Fear not, you worm Jacob, you men of Israel! I will help you, says the Lord; your Redeemer is the Holy One of Israel.
>
> Behold, I will make you to be a new, sharp, threshing instrument which has teeth; you shall thresh the mountains and beat them small and shall make the hills like chaff.
>
> You shall winnow them and the wind shall carry

them away, and the tempest or whirlwind shall scatter them. And you shall rejoice in the Lord, you shall glory in the Holy One of Israel. (Isaiah 41:9-16)

After reading the passage, I felt reassured. *God has called me. He is going to protect me. He'll give me the tools, the words. He'll use me and people like me to cut the abortion clinics out of our society.* Now I use verse 15 of this passage to encourage pro-life groups to unite so that God will use us as a threshing instrument to cut abortion clinics out of our society. Each of us is a tooth in God's threshing machine, a fighter to be used in His battle.

I felt as if the Lord had written the passage just for me. I understood the Lord wanted to take the very worst things in my life and use them for good. I had prayed that He would. My prayer had been, *Use them for Your glory—every filthy thing I have done—please, use it for Your glory, in Your way, not mine.* Testifying in Austin before the legislature was God's way of doing that.

I felt the Lord with me, sitting on that rock in Austin, Texas. When I read those words from the Amplified Bible, I knew God had a plan for me—Carol Everett, sinner extraordinaire...even me. I sat on that rock, crying in amazement that God would use me.

I began to focus on what I would say in the hearing. *I can tell the truth about what I've seen lurking behind those words—"rights" and "choice"—the murdering of babies and maiming of women, even the murder of women. I've witnessed it first-hand. I can tell about botched abortions and the cover-up that goes on behind the closed doors of abortion clinics across the nation. I can tell about 35,000 babies—murdered and ground up like hamburger meat in commercial disposals.*

I marched into the hearing room and testified, absent of the fear I had felt earlier. Yes, I could hear the insults. Sure, I could feel the hatred. No, I did not enjoy the personal attack mounted against me before the legislative committee that day.

But for the first time in my life I was part of a purpose bigger than making money. I was involved in a goal, a worthy goal. Not my goal, but God's goal.

God's Word in Isaiah 41:9-16 challenged me and gave me the courage to serve God as never before.

After I finished testifying, I left the Texas State Capitol, excited that

God had used me. Yes, the Lord could use me in this cause, and I was ready.

Unresolved Guilt

But my enthusiasm quickly dissipated back in Dallas. I still had bills to pay. I was asked to speak and give media interviews, but speaking engagements and interviews didn't pay those bills. I tried once more to make a deal with God. *God, I can dedicate one day a week, maybe two sometimes, to help fight abortion. But love offerings won't take care of my needs.*

As time went on, Jerry and Richard were very understanding and supportive of my pro-life activities. The church prayed faithfully for me. I thought perhaps God was going to let me be successful in real estate leasing, to fight abortion on a limited basis.

Things seemed to be working out just fine—except the more I got involved with pro-life activity, the more often I recalled my own abortion. The more I talked about how things work inside an abortion clinic, the more my insides churned with memories of my abortion.

My private struggle only heightened when Kay Thorogood gave me a gift: a little "precious feet" pin, the international pro-life symbol. I was reluctant to wear it, except to pro-life functions, because it reminded me of my own abortion. I could not openly admit that I had been bad enough to kill my own child. To me, that was an unforgivable sin. I didn't want to tell anyone.

Finally, I tested Jack. "I've got to tell you something, and I hope you won't hate me after I tell you...I had an abortion, and Tom White was the father."

Jack had previously met Tom when he visited the church at my invitation, and had even visited privately with Tom. Now he said to me, "Carol, that makes some things fit together. I can see why you were so open for involvement in the abortion industry. That also explains why you're still so angry at Tom."

He didn't condemn me. He took my revelation matter-of-factly and continued treating me as he always had.

In November, 1985 Barbara, my best friend from the church, called. "Carol, I need to go to Corpus Christi. I bought some antiques from an estate for my store. I need a truck driver! Could you fly down with me Tuesday night and drive back home with me on Wednesday?"

"Yes. I can do that. Let's go." Barbara is such an enjoyable, interesting lady. I was glad to go with her.

We flew to Corpus Christi, where her cousins met us at the airport, fed us dinner, and boarded us for the night. Early the next morning, we picked up our truck, loaded the furniture, and started the ten-hour journey back to Dallas.

Barbara and I had enjoyed another "adventure in moving" a couple of years earlier, when she moved to a house closer to our church. I was the truck driver in that first venture; this time, Barbara wanted to drive. I looked forward to some fun on the way home.

We started off having a great time, talking about anything and everything. During our conversation, we talked about the pro-life movement and about a post-abortive woman I had recently met.

There was a pause in the conversation. Here was my opening. "Barbara, I know how that woman feels. I…had an abortion, too. Tom was the father." For the first time I exposed my private membership in the post-abortive women's society to another woman, a Christian friend.

Silence. I had heard that silence before.

Why doesn't she say something? I never should have told her. I thought I could trust her, but obviously my trust is misplaced—or premature.

I felt rejected. I thought, *If I can't tell Barbara about my abortion, I can't tell anyone. So, I'll have to continue to keep it to myself.*

The rest of the trip seemed to take forever. We had very little conversation the rest of the way home. We delivered the furniture to the shop, and I went home, determined to stop seeing Barbara. *She isn't the friend I thought she was.* My case against her began to build, my old rejection pattern at work again.

After our trip together, I saw Barbara on Sunday, but made sure I was too busy to see her during the week. Things got really tense between us, even to the point of causing conflict between me and her oldest son. I was angry at her, believing she had rejected me. Our relationship was strained until Barbara finally brought Jack into our struggle. He got us together and helped us resolve it.

"Barbara, I thought you were rejecting me when I told you about my abortion on the way back from Corpus Christi," I said.

"Carol, I didn't know what to say to you. I didn't say anything, for fear of saying the wrong thing."

"I am so sorry, Barbara, for the way I've treated you."

It was wonderful to receive her forgiveness. But I still believed most people would not love me or even like me if they knew I had an abortion.

It will stay my secret. No one knows except Jack, Barbara, Tom, Harvey, and me. None of them will tell. My secret is safe. I will never tell anyone else.

A few weeks later, Ron Urban, one of our ministers, asked me, "Carol, will you give a five-minute testimony in our evening service on Sunday?"

"Sure, Ron. I'd love to."

No problem, I thought. *I do that all the time.*

That Sunday afternoon I visited with Barbara, her boys, and some other church members. I spent very little time in prayer or preparation. The testimony wouldn't be any big deal, and I knew it.

Facing My Own Abortion

Sunday night, I stood before my church—the people I loved the most, other than my family.

"I had an abortion."

Where did that come from? The words just slipped out! I told my awful secret to the whole church! I couldn't believe I told them. There must be something about the environment of love and acceptance that permits us to release that old baggage that weights us down.

I was scared, but I proceeded. "I haven't said that before in my testimony. I didn't want to say that." And I started crying.

As I stood there in front of my Christian family, it was as though a spotlight shone directly on my forehead. The big "A" I always imagined there was was back, magnified. Although it had begun to fade when I confessed to God my sin of killing 35,000 babies, at that moment it seemed bigger and brighter than ever before.

My guilt and shame rushed to the surface. "Yes. I had an abortion in 1973. I killed my baby. I have been a member of the secret society of post-abortive women since that time."

Somehow, I got through the rest of my testimony. I thought they would all reject me. They could never love a woman who had killed her baby, could they? It was over. I would have to leave this church and never come back.

But when I stepped down from behind the pulpit, something entirely different happened. They reached out to me—as if they still loved me, no matter what I had done. Person after person, sometimes two at a time, hugged me and cried with me. Standing there in the midst of God's people, with love being lavished on me through my Christian family, the big "A" was washed off my forehead forever.

God forgave me of all my sin when I prayed with Jack the first time, but I was not able to accept it all at once. Acceptance of my redemption came to me a little at a time.

I must tell you, heart to heart; I really believe God washed me in His love—His unconditional love—that night, through the acceptance of His people. I knew that night that the blood of Jesus Christ, shed on the cross for me, covered me completely, all my sin. Before God's people, I stood revealed—the Scarlet Lady, covered in Christ's blood. Not Sheryl's blood, not the blood of 35,000 abortions, and most wonderful of all, not the blood of my child. Not any longer!

> Come now, and let us reason together, says the Lord.
> Though your sins are like scarlet, they shall be as white as
> snow; though they are red like crimson, they shall be like
> wool. (Isaiah 1:18)

On the night I openly confessed to my church, my healing as a post-abortive mother started. I began to cry uncontrollably. Tears flowed non-stop for five months.

When my sister died, there was grief, but it was nothing like the grief that surfaced now. This pain was deeper, a grief from deep, deep down—a guttural grief from the bottom of my soul, a cry that would not stop. It started with a tightness, a knot in my throat that would not allow me to talk without pain.

At pro-life functions I would hear these words over and over: "I just don't understand how a woman could have an abortion. What kind of woman has an abortion? Why does a woman have an abortion? How could any woman have an abortion?"

Secretly, I wondered, "Where is their understanding?" Privately, I was that woman, the kind who would have an abortion.

Now, people asked me those same questions, and I had to provide answers. I desperately wanted to defend post-abortive women, but I had no defense. I even wondered myself, "How? Why?"

After each meeting, I struggled anew with guilt. *I am a murderer. I killed my child, my helpless little baby. If I had only waited, something would have worked out.*

The painful question kept tormenting me. *How could I have done it? I give the impression of being a good mother, but that's a lie. I killed my own baby. Why did I do it? I played God in my life. I chose not to take the gift He gave me.*

I thought about how my life would be different if my third child were alive. I imagined my child with me after his brother and sister were grown and on their own. We would be living together. I would still have at least one child at home to share my life.

At the uttermost depth of my grieving, life did not seem worth living. No, I didn't consider suicide this time, but still there seemed to be no reason to go on. Life was just a pointless, worthless effort.

Those close to me tried to console me. Even George, a dear friend, suggested, "Carol, maybe you need to have a funeral for the baby. I'll go with you. Jack and Gwen will go."

"Thank you, George. That is very kind of you to offer. But I don't think that is necessary."

Work and church became my escapes. Pro-life work was absolution for my sin. Finally, it dawned on me what I was doing. *Why am I punishing myself so?* I prayed and asked God for the answer.

I came to realize that I was punishing myself because I had rejected my own flesh and blood, the gift of love God had given to me. My pattern was always to punish those who reject me until they admit to their offense. Subconsciously, I was punishing myself.

God was freeing me from an old habit pattern that Satan used to destroy me and my relationships.

I prayed for God's help to stop punishing myself and others, to help me stop grieving. I discovered that part of the healing process was to deal with each person involved in my abortion.

I tried to talk to Tom, but he kept saying, "We made the best choice we could at that time. It's behind us now. We have to go on with our lives." Every time I saw him or talked to him on the phone, I brought up the abortion. His answer was always the same. He just couldn't hear my heart.

I struggled with telling Joe Bob and Kelly. *They'll hate me. I swore I would never tell them. But, God, I've told you to use everything from my past life to help others. If this will help Joe Bob and Kelly, I'll tell them.*

I could just hear their questions. Why did you do it? Did you ever think about aborting us? How could you do it? How old would the baby be today?

Joe Bob graduated from the University of Texas on December 18 and married Carol, his longtime sweetheart, December 21. There are two Carol Everetts in the world now, Carol, Junior, and Carol, Senior. I did the best I could to be happy for them, but his leaving home only added to my grieving.

After a lot of inner turmoil I finally resolved I had to tell the children about the abortion.

In March, 1986 both of them were home on the same weekend I was scheduled to speak at the Texas Right to Life Convention in Denton. They agreed to go with me. I tried to tell them the night before, but couldn't. The next morning, things were not right to talk to them. I didn't tell them on the ride to Denton. Before we went into the meeting, I asked them to pray with me, because I knew what I had to do.

When I got up to speak, the knot in my throat was so large I couldn't talk. I finally managed to start. "In 1973, I had an abortion." The lump got smaller. I could not look at my children. I was sure they would hate me.

Tears flooded my eyes. I had to stop to ask the audience to pray with me before I could continue. My children finally knew the deepest, darkest secret about their mother. It was a relief to finally tell them.

I was shocked when they didn't want to talk about it. All they asked was, "Why didn't you tell us?"

And all I could say was, "How does a mother tell an eight and a ten-year-old, 'I just murdered your sibling'?"

They let me off the hook, which, strangely, I regretted. I wanted them to punish me. I wanted to hear them shout, "You made a mistake! You screwed up!" But they were silent, like Tom.

When we left Denton, the knot in my throat was gone forever. And the "precious feet," which before I wore only to pro-life meetings, I now wear daily to remind me of my other child—the third child everyone would now know about.

I didn't yet realize that three major bridges were crossed that day. I told my children about my abortion. I stopped grieving and punishing myself. I also met Jack Wilke, M.D., the president of the National Right to Life organization.

Actively Pro-Life

In the lobby afterward, Dr. Wilke asked for my card and said, "I wondered what changed a woman like you."

How I have grown to love and respect Dr. Wilke and his lovely wife, Barbara! They have given unselfishly of themselves to the pro-life movement. The Lord has mightily used the two of them to do His work and to encourage others like me.

In June, 1986, Dr. Wilke was responsible for my invitation to speak at the National Right to Life Convention in New Orleans. I was well-received in Texas among pro-lifers, but I was nervous about facing the National Convention. I arrived at the convention very early and found my workshop room.

There was a man sitting in the room when I walked in. We struck up a conversation.

"I'm Carol Everett. I am doing the next workshop, and I'm scared no one will come."

"What is the title of the workshop?" Ed, from North Carolina, asked.

"Ex-Abortion Provider Turns Pro-Life." I answered, watching closely for his reaction.

"Oh, your workshop will be well attended. But don't worry; I'll stay just in case no one else comes."

I liked this man. We talked until others started arriving. More and more convention attendees packed the room, until it was standing-room-only. During the meeting, Ed stood up and declared, "This is the best-attended meeting of the convention!" He made me feel so welcome and accepted.

After my appearance at the NRTL Convention, calls for speaking engagements started coming in from all over the nation. I was too busy working with pro-life to continue my job with Richard and Jerry. Richard's prophecy was about to be fulfilled.

Jack and I needed a heart-to-heart talk. "What would you think if I went to work in the pro-life movement, full-time?"

"Carol, prayerfully re-read the Book of Esther," was his advice. I had read it earlier at Jack's direction, but it didn't mean much to me. This time, however, it really spoke to me. Esther was chosen to be queen for her beauty, but God placed her in the palace "for such a time as this." Esther was used by God to deliver her people. She faced danger in that cause, declaring, "If I perish, I perish." Oh, how I identified with that phrase: "for such a time as this"!

I was reminded of the passage in Isaiah and about my time with God on the Capitol steps. I went back to Jack and reported, "I know God means for me to use my life, at this time, to fight abortion. I want to help the world hear the cry of the unborn, saying, 'Let me live.' I know I am intended to go to work as a full-time pro-lifer."

"It's a matter of God's timing, Carol. Let's see what God does next."

Believe it or not, in May we reached a settlement with Harvey Johnson. Jack arranged for the church to receive my part of the monthly settlement. The "blood money" became God's money. With it, the church set up a fund to help fight abortion.

What Would God Do Next?

Another surprise arrived. It was time to trim my household budget, to prepare to live on less income. I got rid of the final items purchased with abortion funds—the sports cars. I sold both cars and signed an unsecured note for more than eleven thousand dollars. The butcher shop closed again, leaving me responsible for a note for fifty-three thousand dollars.

At one time, my total unsecured debt was more than one hundred and fifty-four thousand dollars. Somehow, with the Lord's blessing, in less than three years, my debt was reduced to sixty-four thousand dollars. [At the time of this writing, my debt has been reduced to three thousand six hundred dollars.]

I had learned to work through my trials and not run from them. I knew God had a job for me to do. Somehow, I knew the remaining sixty-four thousand dollars would be managed. I marched ahead with my plan.

In August, 1987, I talked to Jill, assistant to Bill Price, with the Dallas Right-to-Life group. "I want to go into pro-life work full-time," I told her.

She seemed surprised, but said, "I'll mention it to Bill."

In October, Bill Price called. "Could you meet me for lunch, Carol? I'd like to talk to you about coming on staff."

At lunch, Bill said, "I think I can raise the money for you to come on staff, but I can't offer you a position until I do raise the money."

"Is that the way it will be, year after year?" I asked.

"After people have been here a year," he answered, "the money has always come in to allow them to stay. I'm sure it would come in, to keep an ex-abortion provider on the staff of a pro-life group."

After discussing the monetary issue, Bill said, "Carol, there will be times that you won't be able to share your Christian testimony. Times when it won't be appreciated or effective."

"I understand that legislatures don't respect Christian testimony," I replied. "What would I be doing?"

"Pretty much the same thing you're doing now. You'd continue your speaking and educating. Your title would be 'public relations director.' You'd also help me with fund-raising."

"Sounds good to me. Let's see what happens."

In February, 1988, when I went to work full-time with Dallas Right to Life, the *Fort Worth Star-Telegram* did a feature article on me. Tom's mother was still living in Fort Worth. I called Tom and told him what was going to be released, including my acknowledgment of our abortion. I didn't want him or his mother to be surprised by the release. Tom reacted angrily when I told him.

God richly rewarded me throughout the year, with many wonderful experiences and many new friends.

On December 20, I was preparing for a video, to be filmed in our office for Dr D. James Kennedy's ministry, when Bill came in. "Carol, I need to talk to you. I told you that the funds had always come in to keep everyone on staff after their first year. I'm sorry, but the funds have not come in to keep you on staff for another year."

I was stunned.

"Carol, you can stay on and do your own fund-raising. You know it costs an amount equal to your salary for support personnel, office space, and other expenses. You can have ten percent of anything you raise over the seventy-two thousand dollars required."

My initial reaction was, *If I have to raise my own funds, I might as well do it for myself. The Lord is clearly closing this door.* Aloud, I said, "Bill, I'm pretty busy right now with the video. Can we talk about this later?" I was visibly upset.

"Certainly. I'm sorry I had such bad news for you, just before the filming."

In a later meeting, I told Bill, "I want to pray about this over the holidays. I want to be certain where God wants me."

When I returned after the holidays, we met again.

"Bill, I believe I am supposed to resign."

"Carol, if that's what you want to do, I'll pay you for the month of January and you can keep all of your honoraria."

"Thank you, Bill. I really appreciate it."

Where was I to go next? I set up an appointment with Jack to discuss my situation.

"I've decided to leave Dallas Right to Life, and I need some advice."

"Carol, I'll help you set up your own organization if you want. I have extra office space here and will be glad to help you get organized. If you'd like, we could also talk about your joining Marketplace Christian Network."

"I'd rather come under your umbrella, if possible, Jack. I believe that's the best place for me."

Jack and I worked out an agreement which included Charlotte, my assistant at DRTL, joining the MCN staff. In January, 1989, I went to work with Jack as the director of "MCN-ProLife."

15

....

RESTORATION

SOME SAY the day of miracles is past. But I'm living proof that miracles still happen.

In January, 1989, when I went to work with MCN, I was very excited. I kept telling Jack, "I think something really great is about to happen."

"Don't be surprised when it does, Carol."

Jack gave me a minute to try and figure out what he meant. I came up dry.

"The surprise will be what happens, Carol. And the way it happens might even surprise you. Sometimes the surprise is the messenger and sometimes it's the circumstances surrounding the event. You're right, though, Carol; something fantastic is about to happen."

The next two-and-a-half years held many surprises—joyful, peaceful, loving surprises. Fantastic things began to happen in the business, but the real surprises came in the enrichment of relationships.

The Process Begins

On February 16, 1989, I called Tom. "I need to meet with you this morning. I will just take a minute."

"Okay, Carol. Be here at eight o'clock."

I was at Tom's front door at 8:00 A.M. sharp.

"What's so important, Carol Nan?" he asked me when I went inside.

USA Today is coming to the office this morning to interview me about being a post-abortive woman. It's going to be on national television. I wanted to tell you so you wouldn't be be caught off-guard."

"You could have told me that over the telephone. What else is going on?"

I took a deep breath—this was my opening. "Tom, our abortion just about destroyed my life." Tears started to run down my face.

"Well, I guess you think it hasn't affected me," he answered. "It bothers me, too." Tom began to cry along with me; it was the first time I saw Tom hurting over our abortion. For the first time, I realized that Tom gave my feelings some validity. But what about his? I ignored them. I was still struggling too much with my own feelings to be able to reach out to help him.

"Tom, I've got to be free to tell my story. In the future I'm going to tell it, not hold anything back. I hope you can accept it. I want you to release me to do it."

"Okay, Carol. Go ahead."

When I left Tom's house, I felt a lot of relief.

I went to the office and did the interview. A couple of weeks later, Tom called and asked me to do him a favor. "Carol, my car's in the shop. Could you take me to pick it up?"

"Sure, Tom. I'll be happy to."

On the way to pick up his car, I said, "Tom, *USA Today* is showing the interview tonight. I wanted you to know. Will you watch it, so we can talk about it later? I really want your input on how it comes across."

"Okay, Carol Nan."

When I let Tom out of the car, he just stood there. I knew he wanted me to respond to him, but I just drove away. Why didn't I turn around and go back? I just kept driving.

That evening, as soon as *USA Today* was over, I called Tom.

"Did you watch *USA Today?*"

"I didn't get to see all of it. Right in the middle of the show, Mother called. She wasn't happy."

Clearly, it wasn't the right time for Tom and me to talk. At least I didn't think so. Now I realize it would have been the perfect time. Though I didn't fully recognize it, he was struggling with the same rejection I was. We just couldn't help each other at that moment.

A short time later, Tom started dating Sandy. He and Sandy began to visit with Jack at our office. Jack had been helping Tom for some time on how to build better relationships. It really bothered me to see Tom and Sandy come in together.

I set up a meeting with Jack to discuss my feelings. "Why does Tom have to parade Sandy into this office? I think he's doing it just to hurt me."

"Carol, I think you're jealous. Do you still love Tom?" he asked directly. "I think you'd still like to be married to Tom. What do you think?"

"I don't know," I said, not wanting to face his words.

"Why don't we pray about it and find out what the truth is?"

We prayed another one of those killer prayers. Sure enough, I had to admit that in my private heart, the door remained open for Tom to enter. My emotions took off on the same roller coaster ride they had been on throughout our marriage.

And while on that roller coaster, my invisible black slate resurfaced. It had been buried in my memory for years, but it was still intact, with all four of the items still legible:

- Tom believed that children were liabilities rather than assets. That had to change.
- Tom had to accept responsibility for his part in the abortion.
- Tom had to admit he was insensitive to my needs, demonstrated by his failure to ask me if I wanted the child. He had to apologize.
- Tom had to admit that our marriage was only a business arrangement; that he was not a husband to me, just a sex partner and good negotiator.

Not a single one of my conditions had been erased. All of my subconscious thoughts and emotions came out in the open. I had to admit to myself I was still waiting for Tom to realize that I was the only woman who ever truly loved him. I didn't fall into a heap, as his first wife had done; I honored my agreement and aborted our child. It was time we resolved our relationship problems. I felt it could only be accomplished by Tom's admission of his wrongs, his mistakes.

Then I began to realize I was operating on the assumption that God was pleased with my list. I had actually been praying for Tom to meet my subconscious demands. I was playing God, and I was angry because I didn't see Tom turning back to me; he still wasn't cooperating.

I also discovered that I subconsciously believed Tom and I would get back together after the children left home. It would just be Tom and me; the "liabilities" would be gone. I was jealous of Sandy because I thought I should be with Tom. I asked God, "How many more deep roots still bind me to Tom?"

I began to pray. First, I acknowledged to God that Tom was an idol in my life. Then, I asked God to free both of us from my need to punish Tom.

My prayer continued. "God, if You can forgive me for all I've done, You can surely forgive Tom for all he has done, too. And if You can forgive Tom, so can I—and so do I. Help me to remember this prayer and Your love for both of us."

Things began to improve between Tom and I. Finally, in August, I called Tom. "I need to ask you to forgive me, Tom."

"What for, Carol?"

"Tom, I've blamed you for a lot of things—especially the abortion. I've been punishing you for a long time. I'm sorry. Will you forgive me?"

"Yes, Carol. I forgive you. And...will you forgive me for my part in the abortion?"

Did I hear Tom correctly? Did he admit his part in the abortion?

"Yes, Tom. But—it's interesting; you only asked me after I first asked you to forgive me. I wonder...are you sure you mean it? You never called and asked me to forgive you first."

"Hang up the phone, Carol."

"Why, Tom?"

"So I can call you."

I hung up the telephone and waited for it to ring. It did, and I snatched it from the cradle.

"Carol Nan, will you forgive me for my part in the abortion?"

"Yes, Tom. I will. Thank you."

"I love you, Carol."

"I love you, too, Tom."

"Carol, I'll always love you, as long as I live."

"I know, Tom. Good-bye."

I sat in the office, thinking how my whole life was changed after my abortion. And Tom's life had been altered, too. Kelly had been deeply affected; so had Joe Bob. In many ways, we were all victims of that single act of murder.

It's a shame that others have suffered for my sin. It really hurts me that my other children are victims also. They were certainly innocent. Yes, I'm sorry that Tom was hurt by the abortion, but oh, how I wish he had wanted our child! There are so many things I'd like to change, if I could.

But the only change I know I can accomplish is letting the Lord use my experience to show others how destructive abortion is. Maybe I can help others see abortion as a sin. It destroys the family unit, not just the baby and the mother.

By November, I believed Tom was very serious about Sandy. I even called Jack and asked, "Is Tom going to marry Sandy?"

"It looks very serious to me, Carol."

When I hung up the telephone, I was crushed. I thought Tom still loved me. He'd said he would love me forever! My invisible slate still wasn't clean. I knew there was more to be dealt with, but I wasn't willing to pursue the matter at that time. A short time later, Tom and Sandy were married.

Acceptance of Family

Things were relatively quiet in my life for about three months. At one of our regular meetings in May, 1990, Jack asked, "Carol, is it possible the baby you aborted was a little girl, instead of a boy?"

In all of my thoughts, I always had imagined my child was a boy. There had never been a doubt in my mind. "Why in the world did you ask that?" I questioned.

"I've just been wondering. Why do you believe it was a boy?"

"I've never thought about it being a girl. I've always just assumed it was a boy."

I left Jack's office, really disturbed. *What are you trying to do now, God?* (Don't ask that question unless you want to know.)

A few days later, I went back to visit with Jack. "You're exactly right. Today I believe my baby was a little girl, not a boy. It goes back to the way I wished I was a boy, because I thought my father wanted a son so badly. Daddy was my idol, you know. I wanted a boy, especially for Tom, because I idolized Tom, too. I thought the baby boy would be just like his father.

"But I've begun to think of my aborted child as a girl, instead. I've even given her a name—Heidi. Her name means "noble and kind" in German. But to me, her name means "hidden one." She was hidden from me for seventeen years, and she is hidden from the world, but she lives in my heart."

For some reason, a new-found appreciation of myself as a woman was tied to the acceptance of my third child as a little girl. It was as though being a woman took on much greater significance for me.

I remembered the many ways my father treated me like a lady. I realized my daddy really did love me as a woman. He was proud to have two daughters—but I couldn't see it.

On June 2, Joe Bob called. My father was in serious condition. "Gangi is in the hospital in Llano. He's had a heart attack."

"How is he?"

"He's okay, Mom."

"I'll call the hospital, talk to Mother and the doctor, and call you back." When I hung up the telephone, I felt a peace inside, telling me that everything was in good hands. It was going to be all right.

When I reached Mother, she said, "They're going to transfer your daddy to Seton Hospital in Austin and do some more tests."

"He's going to be all right, Mother. I'll talk to the doctor."

I managed to get through to the doctor and got more information.

"Your dad has had a heart attack, but he's going to be fine. I think he has a blockage. We're transferring him to Seton. They'll do tests and probably operate on him within a week."

I called Joe Bob and Kelly and updated them. "I'll see you at the hospital in Austin." I was supposed to fly to Alaska that day, but I postponed the trip and drove to Austin to be with my family.

After the initial tests, the doctors said, "It doesn't look like a heart attack." Two days later they informed us, "He has cancer in his liver and left hip, which can be treated with chemotherapy. He's going to be all right."

I went outside to talk privately with the doctor. "How long does he have?"

"Two years—or longer. It is hard to say."

When I went back into the room, Daddy was crying. I had only seen him cry once before—at Tooter's death. It really upset me. I decided, *I'm going to be strong. He needs me to be strong.* That old pattern surfaced again.

But, this time, God showed me His strength in the midst of my weakness.

Daddy had three chemotherapy treatments and got much better. He was able to go home and go to work again. After several months, though, he started to get worse, but didn't tell anyone. He suffered in silence through five more treatments.

It was hard to work while my daddy was sick, but I managed to continue my speaking schedule. During my times alone, the Lord was really with me, helping me be strong. I prayed so hard for Him to heal my daddy. I interceded in my father's behalf that he might come to know the Lord. I prayed and prayed for God to send someone to talk to him, because I wasn't sure he had things resolved between himself and God.

In the midst of Daddy's illness, Jack and I met with a book publisher for the first time and I agreed to write my life story. I was eager to tell my story, but fearful of the consequences. I didn't know how my family would respond.

Between Daddy's problem and my work on this book, I really focused on family relationships. The children also seemed sensitive to the importance of family. It was the perfect time for God to help us deal with some deep scars caused by my destructive past. I prayed for God to open the opportunity for us to talk about our hurts.

At my birthday dinner in December, Tim, one of Joe Bob's friends, asked me, "What exactly do you do, Mrs. Everett?"

"I work with abortion survivors," I answered.

Joe Bob asked, "What is an abortion survivor?"

"You are an abortion survivor," I answered. "You lost your sister to abortion."

Joe Bob seemed surprised by my response and snapped, "Thank you, Mother."

"Joe Bob, I want you to know I love you very much. You are very special to me. I never considered aborting you."

"Thank you, Mother." This time, Joe Bob's voice was soft and loving.

I don't know if my son ever wondered if I considered aborting him, but I did want him to be sure I never, ever considered it.

Later that evening, in the privacy of my bedroom, I recalled Joe Bob's initial response to my entry into the abortion industry, years earlier. "Abortion is murdering a baby. You shouldn't be in that, Mom."

At that time, I admonished him, "Joe Bob, you'll never get pregnant, and you don't know what it's like. You'll just have to trust me on this one. Go along with me, son."

Joe Bob had no idea how his words that day reminded me that I was indeed a murderer. When I left the abortion industry, Joe Bob commented, "I told you it was wrong, all along."

I don't believe any of us really understand how abortion touches every relationship in our lives—until encouraged to do so.

At my urging, Kelly spent time with Jack, trying to deal with the effects my abortion had on her life, as well as what happened to her while she was in the abortion clinics. Kelly was uniquely affected because I dragged her into the abortion clinics with me; I knew she needed to talk about her time spent in them.

Kelly related these thoughts to Jack:

> I wish I had never worked in an abortion clinic. I was fourteen years old when Mom went to work in the first clinic. I went to work there with her. I did filing, general office work, and answered the telephone.
>
> In the beginning, I believed I was helping the women. But I wasn't. I was so blind about the real issues I was involved with. I believed it was just a fetus—not a baby.
>
> It was hard to walk out in the front of the clinic and see my friends from school—there to have an abortion. They really reacted when they saw me.
>
> Mom was in charge, but Dr. Johnson is the one I performed for. I worked in the clinics for five years and saw a lot. There is no denial anymore about what I saw—I saw body parts in there. Sometimes I think I've had millions of abortions, although I've never personally had one.
>
> I remember a woman who drove a BMW. She had four abortions. She said it was her way of birth control.
>
> One of the things that bothered me the most was the women who were injured. Some of them were retarded women who didn't even realize how they got pregnant. And there were young children who came in who were forced by their parents to have abortions.
>
> I especially remember one "big baby" abortion that was botched [Jenni]. I helped Mother take her to the

hospital. Her bowel was pulled through her uterus. She just kept screaming. It scared me to death.

I thank God I never got pregnant. If I had, I would have had an abortion, too, because in my mind it wasn't a baby. But not today. No, I wouldn't have an abortion today. My opinion has changed drastically. I feel strongly today God chooses for life to begin—He gives life. I am strongly opposed to abortion.

(I thank God, too, Kelly never had an abortion. Also, I am so grateful to God to see that Kelly never really bought into the abortion business, even though I tried to push her into it. She was stronger than her mother.)

Jack also asked Kelly, "Tell me your impressions of your mother today."

When I think about my mother today, I can't help but cry. She is a fighter. She has worked so hard. When we were growing up, she held down two jobs to see that we were taken care of. She would take us home after finishing one job, feed us, and be off to the next job. She is the most dynamic person I know. She's dynamite. I have so much admiration for her.

She thinks she hurt Joe Bob and me—abused us in our childhood. That is not true. She is my very best friend today. Sometimes I tell her things she doesn't like to hear, but I still tell her.

Today, she takes a lot of abuse from the family because of her pro-life work, which is unfortunate. I think she is the greatest.

When I read what Kelly said about me, it just broke my heart. She's probably the person I've hurt the most. It overwhelms me that she can see me the way she does. I messed up so badly, but God has been gracious to me through my daughter's love.

The focus of Kelly's time with Jack changed when he asked, "Kelly, why do you think there wasn't enough room in your home for a little sister?"

There was always enough room as far as I was concerned. Joe Bob and I were told something went wrong with the pregnancy. I never thought Mom had an abortion. When she told me, a few years ago, that she had an abortion, my reaction was, "No, she had a D and C." I still haven't accepted the fact that it was a sibling. I know it is hurting Mom, now. I need to address it. I don't know why she had an abortion. I don't know why!

Kelly is still trying to figure out how her mother, the person she loves and admires so much, could have aborted her sister. That's okay with me, because sometimes I still try to figure it out, too.

Jack and Kelly's time together intensified when Jack asked, "Kelly, if you could change anything today, what would you change?"

I would like to see more emphasis on the family. I wish families cared for one another again—like they once did.

Abortion would be illegal.

I would want my aborted sister to come be with us. I hate to say it, but I've never thought about that before. Recently, a baby in our family was put up for adoption. I wanted to know about that baby. Sitting here, talking to you now, my heart is just breaking for the sibling that was aborted. This is new to me…to think about her being aborted is awful, terrible. Recently, a close friend got pregnant. It made me stop and think. Our aborted sibling never had a chance. It doesn't make much sense.

My entire family would be supportive of my mother. Gangi would be well.

Jack asked Kelly one final question. "Have you ever thought about joining your mother in her crusade?"

Yes. One time she left a message on my answering machine, "I'm scheduled to be on the Capitol lawn at twelve o'clock—Can't make it—will have your speech ready." Mom was teasing, of course, but I didn't think it was funny at the time.

I can't handle the attacks on me right now. I'm not

strong enough to handle them. I hear their lies—I know better.

Probably, I'm a little bit scared too. But it's something we all need to do. I'm scared of standing up there and taking all of the abuse.

I can't think of anyone who would be better to help me than Kelly. She's seen it all, too. I'm waiting for the day we stand beside each other in this fight. Come to think of it—we are, right now!

Letting Go

Dreams only come true in fairy tales. I joined Kelly in wishing Daddy—her "Gangi"—would get well, but his condition worsened. The cancer had increased over 50 percent by early January. He returned to the hospital for three more chemotherapy treatments, which didn't work. The last treatment affected his brain, heart, and liver.

At that time, I told him, "Daddy, I have just one thing I need to talk to you about."

"I'm ready to meet my Maker," he said, but I wasn't so sure he really believed it.

On February 4, the doctor cautioned, "If you want to see your father while he still knows you, I suggest you get here, fast."

I flew to Austin that afternoon and spent the night with my father. My prayer at this time was, "God, tell me when the time is right to talk to Daddy." God hadn't used anyone else to reach my father. Maybe he would use me.

The next day, about half past two, Mother left for a while. Daddy and I were alone. I shared my thoughts with him about Jesus Christ and how I had prayed to receive Him in my heart. When I finished, I asked, "Would you like to pray a prayer and ask Jesus Christ to come into your heart—to be your Lord and Savior?"

"Yes."

I jumped out of the recliner and got on my knees beside his bed. I grabbed Daddy's hand and prayed through tears. "God, I am a sinner. Please forgive me of my sins. Thank you for sending your Son, Jesus Christ, to die for my sins. Reign on the throne of my heart as Lord and Savior. Use my life for your glory. Amen."

When Daddy said, "Amen," I was overjoyed.

Daddy turned his head away from me so I wouldn't see him crying. I knew with all my heart that my father was at the end of himself and that he really wanted to be in heaven.

A peace filled the room. Daddy and I shed tears of joy; I believed Daddy was at peace. He didn't voice another angry word while I was there.

I had to leave on the 8:30 P.M. plane. I touched my father, and I told him I loved him, that I would see him later. I knew, though, it would be the last time I would see Daddy alive.

Right before I left, his kidneys stopped functioning. I shall never forget that look on his face. He knew he was dying, but he didn't fight it. He accepted it. Peace ruled in his heart—and mine.

Mother sat on the other bed and said, "I wish you didn't have to go. Is there any way you can stay?"

Oh, how I wanted to stay! "No, Mother. I'll be back Sunday. I have three speaking engagements that we can't cancel. I love you. Kelly and Joe Bob will be here. I'm sorry I can't stay. Everything is going to be all right." And it was all right!

I returned home to Dallas, very glad and peaceful inside because I knew Daddy was really ready to meet his Maker.

I was in the office the next day when Tom came in to visit with Jack. "How's your dad, Carol Nan?"

"He's dying, Tom."

Tom turned and stumbled out the door. I knew he was crushed. He really did think a lot of my father. I raised my voice and added, "Tom, it's okay. He prayed to receive Christ."

Tom was silent.

It was about noon on Friday, February 8, 1991, when I called from Boston's Logan Airport to find out how Daddy was doing. Joe Bob answered the phone. "Gangi's gone."

"How's Mother?"

"She's fine."

"Let me talk to her."

The first thing she said was, "I'm not going to postpone your father's funeral like I did when Mother died."

"Yes, Mother." Mother's reminder was God's way of showing me how much damage I had done to my mother because of my insensitivity.

It was a big funeral. I thought I'd wandered onto the set of a television show: "This Is Your Life, Carol Nan Everett." Both Jim Bob, my first husband, and Tom were there.

After the funeral, I called to thank Tom for everything he had done for our family during Daddy's illness and death. This time, Tom said to me, "I think of you often, and I pray for you, Carol Nan."

It was so special to hear Tom say those words. I knew he meant them.

"Tom, I want you to know I'm praying for you and Sandy. I want you to be happy."

After the funeral, I spent some wonderful time alone with my mother. I came away with a whole new perspective of her: I did not see her as weak anymore. She's strong and she's been very strong for years—I just couldn't see it.

I want to get to know her much better. The jealousy is gone, maybe because Daddy isn't between us anymore.

God Is at Work

Things settled back down after Daddy's death, and I got back to work on the book and other things. Jack came in one day and announced, "Tom is agreeable to being interviewed about his part in the abortion and having it included in the book."

"I knew all along Tom was going to have his part in the book," I admitted.

I was anxious to hear the results of Jack's visit with Tom. In the interview, Jack asked Tom, "What impact do you think the abortion had on your marriage?"

> I wasn't aware of any impact at that time. Now, I know it was devastating. But we didn't have a marriage, at least not a marriage as I understand marriage today. We had an agreed-upon arrangement. The impact on the arrangement was minimal, however, because Carol couldn't talk to me about it.
>
> She came in one day and said, "I'm pregnant." I didn't react or say anything. She proceeded to carry out our agreement. I didn't challenge it, but I wasn't comfortable with it, either. I couldn't tell her. I didn't stop it,

though, because it was a part of my deal. We had agreed if she got pregnant, she would have an abortion. I believed both of us should uphold our part of the agreement. I'm still a little bit that way.

Both of us got married too quickly our first times because of crisis pregnancies. Carol Nan was pregnant and Susan, my first wife-to-be, was too. We had children too early. Each of us believed marriage was forever, and we had failed in our first marriages. Both of us felt guilty for the mess we made with our first spouses.

I didn't want the responsibility of another child. We made the decision, as we knew it, with the heartache we had been through. But it was a mistake.

I guess every person plays the game of "what if," going back through past times in life. "What if things had been different?" I'm no different. A part of the reason why this reflection appeals to me now is the opportunity to learn more about building relationships based on trust. I've learned to trust people in my professional life, but I have been unable to trust in my personal life until recently.

Rather than carrying a shield to protect my past hurts, I want to trust, to be able to deal openly with all the cards dealt me. If only I had been able to let go and trust in my past, how much different my life would have been.

Carol and I were really volatile together in many respects. We couldn't work through our problems, and the baby was just another problem.

I have asked God to forgive me many times. The issue of children has been very confusing to me. Today, I clearly see what role children play in life. I have cheated myself out of the frustration and joy of raising children.

It's a control issue. I was in control. If it's really God's plan to give us children, then I've missed a part of my life. Remember, I do have a son, though. My life is not through. Children will surface again in my life.

I won't have any more biological children, but we

will come up with more children in our lives. Maybe foster children. My wife is a teacher. She does really well with children. I don't know how good a father I'll be this time, though.

I've asked Carol to forgive me for it a couple of times, but I'm still not sure she has. Sometimes her actions still make me wonder. I can't go back and change what I did. I've asked God to forgive me.

"Tom, what message do you have for men who are facing their participation or the possibility of their participation in an abortion?"

It comes back to an issue of control. Before you decide to terminate the pregnancy, it's important to understand why you are considering doing it. It's probably for reasons you're unable to voice. You may not be very risk-oriented, but having the baby is well worth the risk.

And I have some questions for men, like me, who have participated in abortions. Why did you participate? How has your value system changed since you aborted your child? What is your relationship with the person you were involved with in aborting the child? How do you deal with the fact your parents didn't abort you? How do you live with what you've done? These are some of the questions I have struggled with, myself.

I can tell you I've made my bed, and now I live with the emptiness, amidst tears, particularly when I see the joy children bring to their parents and other people.

When I finished digesting Tom's remarks from his interview with Jack, I realized, *God is at work, changing Tom, too.* I told myself I have to focus on the new Tom that is evolving, rather than the old Tom I knew. I am so glad God doesn't freeze us in our mistakes, but instead warmly, lovingly changes us. I silently prayed, *Lord, help me to see and love the man You are making Tom into today.*

The world tells a woman there's something wrong with her if she has an emotional problem with her abortion. After all, the woman is supposed to be liberated from having to carry a child for nine months when she has an abortion. So, the woman tends to push aside her feelings of remorse. She tries to convince herself that "abortion is the best thing that ever happened to me." The denial period can last for years.

But think of what the man must go through. If the woman is not supposed to be hurt by the abortion, the man certainly is not supposed to be hurt. He, too, suppresses his feelings for years. Tom was no exception. It has taken him eighteen years to begin to work through his true feelings.

I could not finish this chapter without telling you how God has changed my heart toward Harvey Johnson. Yes, there was a time when I wanted to hurt Harvey as badly as he hurt me. Now, I know revenge is not mine. I know God is working with Harvey and Fredi, too.

I pray that they come to know the Lord. I would love for Harvey to become a pro-lifer, actively involved in fighting abortion. That may or may not happen. I know Harvey has a real Christian friend in Wayne Byles, who has not given up on prayerfully trying to help him get out of the abortion business. I pray Wayne is successful.

I ask you to please indulge me now, while I write a few words to my unborn daughter:

> Heidi, I wish I could see you right now and hold you. But, for now I can only share with you what's on my heart.
>
> I hope you like the name I've given you. Precious one, you were hidden from me for seventeen years. I'm sorry it took me so long to acknowledge you.
>
> Although you have never physically lived on this earth, you have lived for more than eighteen years in my heart. It's true, your father and I had no place for you in our home, but you have always had a home in my heart. You will live there as long as I live. I wear my gold, "precious feet" pin everywhere I go to remind me of you.
>
> Heidi, nothing can replace the loss of you. But I want you to know your death has not been without purpose. The love God has shown to me in forgiving me compels me to work hard, telling every mother and father I can about my mistake. I try to help them hear the cry of their unborn child, saying, "I want to live. I want to have a chance to grow to my full potential. Don't shut me out before I have an opportunity to share my life with you. Don't shut your heart to me."

I'm also trying to help all of the families who have been damaged by abortion. I want them to discover the power of love that I know today and continue to see working in our family.

Heidi, I look forward to seeing you in heaven, in your home. I know you and your Aunt Tooter, Gangi, and our other loved ones are already there, having a glorious time.

Heidi, you'd be graduating from high school this year and preparing to go off to college. I'd be helping you select a college, just like I did with your brother and sister. They'd be right in the middle, helping us with your selection! You'd really love Joe Bob and Kelly—as I do.

I have a special request to make of you, one which I think you can honor. Please sing a song to the Lord—a joyful song of thanksgiving for all the love He's shown to our family.

Heidi, I love you, and miss you with all my heart. I can hardly wait to hug you and join you in our heavenly home.

To say I have been surprised by the events of the past two-and-a-half years is an understatement. The greatest surprise is the miracle of how God has changed my heart and is working in all my relationships. He is creating the desire in me to love people I formerly hated, and to forgive others as He forgives me. This is indeed a miracle.

I have been blessed beyond measure from the moment I prayed with Jack, "God, I've been running my own life and have missed the mark You intended me to hit. Father, thank You for sending Your Son, Jesus Christ, to die for my sins. Thank You for raising Him from the dead and making Him living Lord over all. Come into my heart, Lord Jesus, and begin to reign over my life. Begin to love through me as only You can, and make me a worker in Your vineyard. Amen."

I exchanged thirty-eight years of destructive living for life as a worker in God's vineyard. I thank You, Lord, for the privilege of being a tine in Your winnowing fork, being used to cut abortion clinics out of our society forever.

Inside, I hear a voice saying, *The best is yet to be.*